Life of Fred

Jelly Beans

Life of Fred
Jelly Beans

Stanley F. Schmidt, Ph.D.

Polka Dot Publishing

ISBN: 978-1-937032-03-6

Library of Congress Catalog Number: 2011961401
Printed and bound in the United States of America

Polka Dot Publishing   Reno, Nevada

To order copies of books in the Life of Fred series,

visit our website PolkaDotPublishing.com

Questions or comments? Email Polka Dot Publishing at lifeoffred@yahoo.com

Second printing

Life of Fred: Jelly Beans was illustrated by the author with additional clip art furnished under
license from Nova Development Corporation, which holds the copyright to that art.

for Goodness' sake

or as J.S. Bach—who was
never noted for his plain
English—often expressed it:

Ad Majorem Dei Gloriam
(to the greater glory of God)

If you happen to spot an error that the author, the publisher, and the printer missed, please let us know with an email to: lifeoffred@yahoo.com

As a reward, we'll email back to you a list of all the corrections that readers have reported.

A Note Before We Begin
Life of Fred: Jelly Beans

In the twinkling of an eye, forty years pass.

What seems like a second ago, my daughter looked out a window of our home. Today she takes her daughter to ballet class.

When I took this picture, there was *film* in the camera. Black-and-white film. I developed the film and printed this picture in a darkroom.

WOULD YOU CARE TO TRY AND PREDICT THE FUTURE?

And yet, every parent must try.

For each parent's job is to prepare their children for their future lives as adults. Two hundred years ago, this was much easier to do. In those days the next twenty years were a lot like the previous twenty years.

Today, the future is almost unknowable.

It is very dangerous, especially in writing, to predict the future but I am a fool and will try. Here are three things I anticipate that won't go out of style for your children: hugs, kisses, and mathematics.

Let's make a deal: You provide the first two, and I'll supply the last one.

All the best to you.

Stan

HOW THIS BOOK IS ORGANIZED

Each chapter is about six pages. At the end of each chapter, except the last, is a Your Turn to Play.

Have a paper and pencil handy before you sit down to read.

Each Your Turn to Play consists of about four or five questions. Have your child write out the answers—not just orally answer them.

After all the questions are answered, then take a peek at my answers that are given on the next page. At this point your child has *earned* the right to go on to the next chapter.

Don't just read the questions and look at the answers. Your child won't learn as much taking that shortcut.

Contents

10

Chapter One
To Fritter

 red loved speaking to large groups. Over the years that he had taught at KITTENS University, he had classes of all sizes. His beginning algebra classes often had hundreds of students.

It was about one o'clock in the afternoon when he received an invitation from Polka Dot Publishing to be the keynote speaker at the Math and Pizza Conference at 4 p.m.

He had three hours to prepare a 45-minute speech on any math or pizza topic.

Did Fred spend those 180 minutes carefully preparing his presentation? No.

$$\begin{array}{r} 60 \ \text{minutes/hour} \\ \times\ 3 \ \text{hours} \\ \hline 180 \end{array}$$

Did he sit down and write an outline of his talk? No.

Instead, Fred spent . . .

✳ about 25 minutes deciding which bow tie and which pair of shoes to wear.

✳ some time talking with Betty and Alexander about how clean his sleeping bag was, about the honey cards he had invented, about where bees make their hives, and about the countries surrounding the Mediterranean Sea.

✻ minutes going crazy about ice cream.

✻ about an hour at the shopping mall picking out an ice cream maker.

✻ about twenty minutes at the grocery store buying the ingredients for the ice cream maker.

✻ ten minutes helping Stanthony determine the perimeter of his restaurant for Christmas lights.

At 3:05 he climbed on top of the ice cream machine and found the instruction manual. After getting the machine started, he wandered over to the Pizza Buttons booth and bought some buttons. By about 3:40 the ice cream had been served. Fred visited the Brass Braces booth and bought some braces. Fred ordered his pizza. At five minutes to four, he stopped in front of a television and watched part of a Marx Brothers' movie.

At four o'clock he walked up to the speaker's platform and greeted Elaine Marie. Polka Dot Publishing had sent her to the Math and Pizza Conference to act as master of ceremonies.

He straightened his pink bow tie and told Elaine Marie that his speech was going to be on ice cream.

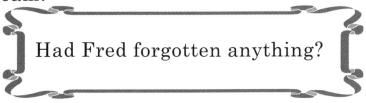

Had Fred forgotten anything?

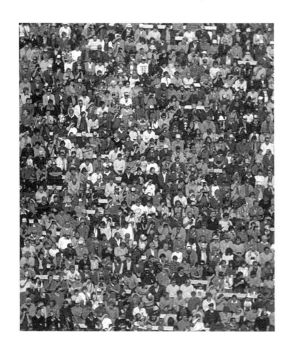

She addressed the conference, "It gives me great pleasure to introduce our keynote speaker for our Math and Pizza Conference. Fred Gauss will be speaking on the topic of ice cream."

Fred was surprised. Usually, introductions of the keynote speakers take five or ten minutes. That would have given him a little time to think about what he was going to say. Instead, he heard polite applause and the room became very quiet.

The spotlight was on him and he felt like he was one inch tall. ⇨

Fred had frittered away those three hours that he had to prepare his speech. One by one he had wasted those 180 minutes.

small essay

How to Fritter

Little babies can't fritter away anything. They spend 100% of their time doing exactly what they are supposed to be doing: eating, crawling around, playing with their toes, and sleeping.

When you grow up, there are two things you can fritter away: your money and your time.

Spend your money on little trinkets and bibelots, and suddenly you find you can't pay the rent.

Waste your time—there are a thousand ways to do that—and suddenly you find that your tombstone will read: I just amused myself my whole life.

end of small essay

Fred swallowed hard. He didn't know how to begin.

He thought of just saying, "Hi!" and waving. But that would be very juvenile (kid-like).

He thought of saying the usual thing that many speakers say, "I'm so glad to be here today. I want to thank Polka Dot Publishing for giving me this opportunity to be your keynote speaker." But that would just waste time.

Instead, Fred began boldly with, "Ice cream."

Your Turn to Play

1. Out of the 800 in the audience, 197 of them had already eaten at least a quart of ice cream. At this point, they were only mildly interested in the topic of ice cream. But for the rest of those 800 people, Fred's words were the most electrifying beginning of a math-and-pizza speech that they had ever heard. How many of the 800 were in this second category?

2. Babies can't fritter away their time. Suppose you have 82 years in your life after you stopped being a baby. How many days would that be? (Let's say that there are 365 days in a year.)

3. Joe spends 62 hours each month watching television. If half of that time is wasted, how many hours has he frittered away each month? (Hint: to find half of something, divide it by 2.)

4. Darlene sleeps about one-third of each 24-hour day. How many hours is that?

5. In the last 17 months, how many months has Darlene slept? (Hint: the answer is going to be 5⅔ months.)

. . . . . . .ANSWERS . . . .

1.   800   in the audience
   − 197   who are only mildly interested
    603   who are really interested

2. 82 years and 365 days in a year—do we add, subtract, multiply, or divide?

   We restate the problem with simple numbers. Suppose we have 4 years and there are 3 days in a year. Then 4 years would be 12 days. We multiplied.

$$
\begin{array}{r}
365 \\
\times\ 82 \\
\hline
730 \\
2920 \\
\hline
29930
\end{array}
$$

There are 29,930 days in 82 years.

3. Half of 62. . . . .

$$
\begin{array}{r}
31 \\
2\overline{)\,62} \\
6 \\
\hline
02 \\
2 \\
\hline
0
\end{array}
$$

He fritters away 31 hours each month.

4.

$$
\begin{array}{r}
8 \\
3\overline{)\,24} \\
24
\end{array}
$$

She sleeps 8 hours each day.

5. One-third of 17. . . . .

$$
\begin{array}{r}
5\frac{2}{3} \\
3\overline{)\,17} \\
15 \\
\hline
2
\end{array}
$$

Chapter Two
Breaking Tradition

The audience was stunned. At the previous 39 Math and Pizza Conferences, the keynote speaker had talked about either math or pizza.

Some Previous Topics

1892: The history of math in 45 minutes.*

1896: If you had an infinite number of pizzas (which you numbered 1, 2, 3, 4, . . .) and each pizza had an infinite number of pepperoni slices is there a way you could number each of the slices so that none of them would be left out?**

_____

* See *Life of Fred: Advanced Algebra*, pp. 52–63.

** If you just started numbering the slices on the first pizza, then the slices on the second pizza would never receive a number.

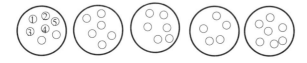

If you called the first slice on the first pizza "1", and the first slice on the second pizza "2", and the first slice on the third pizza "3", then the second slice on the first pizza would never get a number.

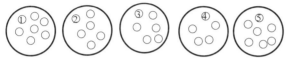

When Fred tells the story of the Big Motel to the seven Dust Bunnies in Chapter 7 of *Life of Fred: Advanced Algebra*, he shows how it can be done. In that story, there are an infinite number of buses, and each bus contains an infinite number of people.

1900: You take a little survey of how men and women pay for their pizzas at PieOne. Six women paid in cash and three paid with a credit card. Nine men paid in cash and five with a credit card. What is the probability that there is no difference in paying patterns between women and men?*

Prof. Eldwood raised his hand and asked, "Excuse me, sonny. Are you breaking tradition? I thought you said 'Ice cream.' Did I hear you correctly?"

Here was the perfect opportunity for Fred to change the topic of his talk. He could have told Prof. Eldwood, "No. I didn't say 'Ice cream.' I started to say, '*I seem* to have so much to talk about."

Ice cream and *I seem* do sound a lot alike.

But that would have been lying, and Fred doesn't lie.

Fred answered, "Yes. I said, 'Ice cream,' and. . . ."

A three-year-old came up and tugged on Fred's shirt sleeve. She was taller than Fred. She had heard Fred correctly. Kids often have better hearing than old men. She asked, "Are you an ice cream man?"

Her embarrassed mother came, picked her up, and took her back to her seat.

───────────────

* That's a tough question. Very few people know that they should use Fisher's Exact test to find out that there is a 63.26% probability that the paying patterns are the same. *Life of Fred: Statistics*, pp. 254–255.

Fred needed a little more time to think. He asked Elaine Marie if he could have something to write on.

She said, "I brought a white board. It's right behind you." She handed Fred a dry erase marker.

Fred wrote: **ice cream**. And then he erased it. Prof. Eldwood had written in his notes: *ice cream*. And then he crossed it out: *ice cream*.

Fred announced that he would start at the beginning and wrote: **My ice cream**.

Joe turned to Darlene and asked, "Is this math or pizza?"

Fred had overheard Joe and said, "This is math." He wrote another word: **My ice cream excises**.

Joe put up his hand and said, "You misspelled *exercise*."

Darlene poked Joe in the ribs and told him that *excises* means to get rid of or cut out. Doctors excise tumors. Authors excise sentences from their manuscripts.

Prof. Eldwood was unhappy that Joe was talking so much. It made it hard to concentrate on what Fred was saying.

Fred was delighted that Joe was slowing things down. It gave him more time to think. He wrote: **My ice cream excises politicians' multitudinous**.

✳ Elaine Marie wondered how this was all going to turn out. Would this be the last Math and Pizza Conference?

✳ Prof. Eldwood wrote with his fountain pen: *My ice cream excises politicians' multitudinous*.

✳ Joe wrote: *My ice cream excises politician's multitudinous*. In Joe's usual loud voice he told Darlene, "Fred made another mistake. He got the apostrophe in the wrong spot."*

✳ At the same time, Betty and Alexander both figured out what Fred was doing. They applauded. And they both wondered what 17-letter word Fred was going to use to finish his sentence.

✳ Joe asked Darlene what *multitudinous* meant. She told him that it had something to do with being a multitude. She then explained that a multitude means a great number or numerous. Joe crossed out ~~multitudinous~~ and wrote *many*.

---

* Joe was wrong. Normally to indicate the **possessive case**, you add an apostrophe and an -*s*. John's hat. Children's section. Iris's dress.

But if it is plural and if it ends in -*s*, then you just add an apostrophe. Mathematicians' joy. Voters' right to secrecy. Dancers' costumes.

Your Turn to Play

1. Betty and Alexander recognized that Fred was creating a sequence. Some sequences are easy to recognize.

    Give the next three terms of 2, 4, 6, 8, _?_, _?_, _?_.

2. How many of these sequences can you recognize? (Few readers will get them all.)

a) 3, 6, 9, 12, 15, _?_, _?_, _?_.

b) 20, 200, 2,000, _?_, _?_, _?_.

c) 1, 0, 2, 0, 3, 0, 4, 0, _?_, _?_, _?_.

d) 1, 2, 4, 7, 11, 16, 22, 29, 37, _?_, _?_, _?_.

e) 1, 12, 123, 1234, _?_, _?_, _?_.

f) 427, 427, 427, 427, _?_, _?_, _?_.

g) 1, 1, 2, 3, 5, 8, 13, 21, 34, _?_, _?_, _?_.

3. Fred had written **My ice cream excises politicians' multitudinous.** If you count the number of letters in each word: 2, 3, 5, 7, 11, 13, you have a sequence. These numbers are special numbers. Each of them have *exactly two divisors*. Take 7, for example. The two numbers that can divide evenly into 7 are 1 and 7. No other numbers divide evenly into 7. If I try to divide 2 into 7, I get a remainder:

$$2\overline{)7}\begin{array}{r}3\,R1\\\hline\\6\\\hline 1\end{array}$$

2, 3, 5, 7, 11, 13 are called **prime numbers**. Name the next prime number after 13.

.... ANSWERS ....

1. 2, 4, 6, 8, 10, 12, 14. These are the even natural numbers.

2.

a) 3, 6, 9, 12, 15, 18, 21, 24. Add 3 to the previous number.

b) 20, 200, 2,000, 20,000, 200,000, 2,000,000. Multiply the previous number by 10.

c) 1, 0, 2, 0, 3, 0, 4, 0, 5, 0, 6. Alternate between the natural numbers and zero.

d) 1, 2, 4, 7, 11, 16, 22, 29, 37, 46, 56, 67. Add 1 to the first number to get the second. Add 2 to the second number to get the third. Add 3 to the third number to get the fourth. (In algebra, you would say, "Add n to the nth number to get the $n+1^{st}$ number.")

e) 1, 12, 123, 1234, 12345, 123456, 1234567.

f) 427, 427, 427, 427, 427, 427, 427.

g) 1, 1, 2, 3, 5, 8, 13, 21, 34, 55, 89, 144. These are called the Fibonacci numbers. (fib-ann-NAH-chee) Each term in the sequence is the sum of the two previous terms. For example, 13 is the sum of 5 and 8. Fibonacci wrote about this sequence in 1202. That's before your parents were born. The Fibonacci numbers are so important that you can subscribe to *The Fibonacci Quarterly*, which has been published since 1963.

3.

14 isn't the next prime number because it has four divisors: 1, 2, 7, 14.

15 isn't the next prime number because it has four divisors: 1, 3, 5, 15.

16 isn't the next prime number because it has five divisors: 1, 2, 4, 8, 16.

17 is prime. Only 1 and 17 divide evenly into it.

Chapter Three
Finishing the Sentence

Fred was starting to sweat. He had written **My[2] ice[3] cream[5] excises[7] politicians'[11] multitudinous[13]** and now he had to find a 17-letter word to finish the sentence.

Here are Fred's thoughts:

That last word had to be a **noun** (a person, place, or thing) in order to make sense. So far, the sentence he had written meant that his ice cream would get rid of politicians' many. . . .

That noun had to be plural (more than one), because of the word *multitudinous*.

What do politicians do? They fight with each other. *Wars* would work, except that it isn't 17 letters long.

They dispute. But *disputes* isn't 17 letters long.

They argue. But *arguments* isn't 17 letters long.

They strive with each other. But *strivings* isn't 17 letters long.

They contend with each other. They are contentious. (*Contentious* is an adjective—it describes.) The noun would be *contentiousness*—the state of wanting to argue. It has 15 letters. I need the plural. Yes!

Fred finished his sentence: **My ice cream excises politicians' multitudinous contentiousnesses**. 2, 3, 5, 7, 11, 13, and 17.

Joe asked Darlene what it meant. She told him that if you feed ice cream to politicians, then they will fight less.

Betty telephoned the company that publishes lists of world records. She told them that Fred had created the world's longest prime number sentence.*

Everyone at the conference stood up and applauded. Joe stood up and clapped because everyone else was doing that.

One man ran up and shook Fred's little hand. That was a mistake. Fred was still holding the dry erase marker in his hand.

Fred was exhausted. It had been a long time since he had worked that hard. His pink bow tie was crooked.

Elaine Marie told him that his speech was magnificent. She told him that Polka Dot Publishing would be happy to invite him back to the next conference in four years.

Fred said that he would be delighted. He promised himself that next time he wouldn't fritter away the time before his speech. He would be prepared.

Stanley Anthony came in from his kitchen and announced, "Your

---

* The previous record was: He ate pizza. 2, 3, 5

pizzas are now ready. If everyone would please take a seat, I will serve them to you."

He handed a pizza to Sam and said, "Enjoy your pizza, Sam." And then one to Tracy and said, "Enjoy your pizza, Tracy." Then one to Shirley, then to Jean, to Shelly, to Drew, to Cameron, to Jan, to Pat, to Robin. . . .

Fred was amazed and wondered *How did Stanthony remember who ordered which pizza? And how did he remember all their names? When he took their orders, most of the people were just standing around, so he hadn't just written down which table they were sitting at.*

If everyone were from KITTENS University, then he would have learned their names over the years but many of these people had come from other states and other countries.

Life is full of mysteries—some of which we solve, and some of which never get explained.

Most of the seats were taken. Fred found an empty one, sat down, and closed his eyes for a second. It had been a busy Sunday.

Giving the keynote speech was the last thing on his schedule today. He could relax now.

He felt someone pulling on his sleeve. He didn't want to open his eyes.

"Hey, Mr. Man." It was the three-year old. "I heard you talk about it—about ice cream. Have you met my dolly? You are a very short man—or are you a boy?"*

Fred answered, "Yes I did. No. Boy."

The three-year-old didn't understand Fred's answers because she wasn't even listening to her own questions.

Lacking another segue, she held up her doll and said, "This is Raggy. She's my Rag-A-Fluffy doll."

Raggy

Fred had heard about Rag-A-Fluffy dolls but had never seen one. He asked, "How can you tell whether it was a boy doll or a girl doll?"

"My mommy said that I could pick."

Fred thought to himself, *It's amazing how a person's speech changes as he/she grows up.*

Three-year-old: I could pick.
Six-year-old: I could chose which one.
13-year-old: R U Cra-Z?

---

* The speech of three-year-olds can sometimes be difficult to listen to if you are tired. She offered no segue (SAY-gway) between ice cream, her dolly, and Fred's shortness. There was no smooth transition (= segue).

Segue comes from the Italian word *seguire* which means to follow or to continue.

In adult conversation, you add in words to indicate you are changing the topic. You might say, "I heard you talk about ice cream. *And, by the way,* have you met my dolly?"

College graduate (from a good college): My mother informed me that I could select the gender of my soi-disant *child.*
    Joe: I thought they were all girl dolls.
    Darlene: My doll (thinking of Joe) is a boy doll.

Your Turn to Play

1. "I told my mommy that I wanted 25 Rag-A-Fluffy dolls. She said that'd cost a million dollars." How much would each doll cost?

2. Prime numbers are numbers that have exactly two divisors. Find the next three prime numbers after 17.

3. Prof. Eldwood knew that just writing *My ice cream excises politicians' multitudinous contentiousnesses*, would not be enough to fill a book. He wrote about a function with a domain equal to the set of all words and a codomain equal to the set of natural numbers, {1, 2, 3, 4, 5, 6, . . .}.

    With his fountain pen, he wrote *my* → *2, ice* → *3, cream* → *5.* What number would *Fred* be mapped to?

4. [hard question] One fourth of all adults can show/prove/argue that no even number larger than 2 can be a prime number. Do you have any thoughts as to why 9296292399773472234292614 (which is an even number) can't be prime?

5. Let's play You Are the Author.™ How would *you* explain how Stanthony delivered each pizza to the correct person? Feel free to invent any story you like.

......ANSWERS ....

1. We are given: 25 dolls cost $1,000,000. Do we add, subtract, multiply, or divide? If you are not sure, then restate the problem with easier numbers. Suppose 2 dolls cost $6. Then each one would cost $3. You divided.

$$25\overline{)1000000} \quad \begin{array}{r} 40000 \\ \hline \end{array}$$
$$\underline{100}$$

Each doll would cost $40,000.

2. 18 won't work. It has 6 numbers that divide evenly into it: 1, 2, 3, 6, 9, 18.

19 works.

20 won't work. It has 6 numbers that divide evenly into it: 1, 2, 4, 5, 10, 20.

21 won't work. It has 4 numbers that divide evenly into it: 1, 3, 7, 21.

22 won't work. It has 4 numbers that divide evenly into it: 1, 2, 11, 22.

23 works.

24 won't work. It has 8 numbers that divide evenly into it: 1, 2, 3, 4, 6, 8, 12, 24.

25 won't work. It has 3 numbers that divide evenly into it: 1, 5, 25.

26 won't work. It has 4 numbers that divide evenly into it: 1, 2, 13, 26.

27 won't work. It has 4 numbers that divide evenly into it: 1, 3, 9, 27.

28 won't work. It has 6 numbers that divide evenly into it: 1, 2, 4, 7, 14, 28.

29 works.

3. *Fred* would be mapped to 4 since it has four letters.

4. *An argument showing that no even number larger than 2 can be prime:* Any even number larger than 2, such as 929629239977347223429261 4 must have at least three numbers that divide evenly into it. Namely, 1, 2 and the number itself.

5. Your answer may be different than mine.

Possibility #1: When Stanthony took each order, he copied their name from their name tag and then drew a picture of the person on the order.

Possibility #2: He was very good at memorizing names and faces.

Possibility #3: He took a picture of the whole crowd (like the one on page 15) and labeled each person in the picture with their name and order number.

Possibility #4: He pasted each person's name and order number on their back.

Chapter Four
What Raggy Taught Fred

Remember the Honey Cards that you did before starting each chapter? As I promised, you don't have to do them any more.

They are not obligatory. But, maybe, they would be nice. ☺

Fred watched as the three-year-old stuck a giant pacifier into her doll's mouth. She explained that the pacifier kept Raggy from crying.

He thought about his own doll, Kingie. When Kingie was new, he didn't say much, and he didn't do much. Now, five years later, Kingie was an internationally recognized artist, and he expressed opinions about lots of things, including which pets Fred should own.

Fred suddenly realized: *Some dolls can grow up!* He wondered why he had never thought of that. No book he had ever read mentioned that. Nobody he knew talked about that. Fred was flabbergasted.*

And what really made Fred's heart beat faster was when he wondered: *How many things are there in life for me to learn? What surprises await me?*

---

* Flabbergasted = overcome with amazement, bowled over, surprised, astounded.

Fred had seen a lot of surprises in mathematics but in the rest of life, he was a mere five-year-old.

He knew about **casting out nines** but he didn't have a clue what it felt like to be 70.

small essay
How to Cast out Nines and Why

Take any number, say, 873. Add the digits together: 8 + 7 + 3 = 18.

Add them together again: 1 + 8 = 9.

You keep doing that until you get a single-digit answer. That's how you cast out nines.

If you know how to cast out nines, you can check the answers to giant multiplication problems very quickly.

Suppose someone tells you that 83954 × 6728 equals 564,842,712. (This answer is too large for many calculators.) You cast out nines for each of these three numbers and do the problem with the one-digit numbers.

83954 ⇒ 8+3+9+5+4 = 29   2+9 = 11   1+1 = <u>**2**</u>

6728 ⇒ 6+7+2+8 = 23   2+3 = <u>**5**</u>

564842712 ⇒ 5+6+4+8+4+2+7+1+2 = 39   3+9 = 12   1+2 = <u>**3**</u>

Does 2 × 5 = 10 ⇒ 1+0 = 1 equal 3? No. We can say for certain that the answer is wrong.

Casting out nines will catch about 90% of the errors (90 out of a 100).

Of course, you could always just multiply it out to check whether 83954 × 6728 equals 564,842,712.

$$\begin{array}{r} 83954 \\ \times\ \ 6728 \\ \hline 671632 \\ 167908 \\ 587678 \\ 503724\ \ \ \ \ \\ \hline 564842512 \end{array}$$ and this is not equal
to 564,842,$\underline{7}$12.

end of small essay

In Fred's Advanced Algebra class, he would amaze his students by showing them how to get the answer to 7^{1000} in three steps.

7^{1000} is "seven raised to the 1000th power" which is 7 × 7 × 7 × 7 × 7 × 7 × 7 × 7 × 7 × 7 × 7

That would take several hours to do with a calculator and a month to do with paper and pencil.

This can all be done in three steps: ① Take the log of 7. ② Multiply by 1000. ③ Take the antilog.

To take the log of a number you need a scientific calculator, which costs about ten or fifteen dollars. You type in 7 and hit the log key. Out comes 0.845098040014256830712216. You multiply that by a thousand (move the decimal over three places) and get 845.098040014256830712216. And then take the antilog (by hitting two keys on the calculator) and get 1.253256639965718318107 times 10^{845} which is 1253256639965718318107000000000000000000000000000 00000000000000000000000000000000000000000000000000000000000000000000000000000000000000 00000000000000000000000000000000000000000000000000000000000000000000000000000000000000 00000000000000000000000000000000000000000000000000000000000000000000000000000000000000 00000000000000000000000000000000000000000000000000000000000000000000000000000000000000 00000000000000000000000000000000000000000000000000000000000000000000000000000000000000 00000000000000000000000000000000000000000000000000000000000000000000000000000000000000 00000000000000000000000000000000000000000000000000000000000000000000000000000000000000 00000000000000000000000000000000000000000000000000000000000000000000000000000000000000 00000000000000000000000000000000000000000000000000000000000000000000000000000000000000 00000000000000000000000000000000000000000000000000000000000000000.

All this will be explained v e r y s l o w l y when we get to advanced algebra. Right now, just appreciate that you can find the product of one thousand 7s (which is 7^{1000}) in only three steps.

There are many flabbergasting things awaiting you in math and in all of life.

Your Turn to Play

1. Use casting out nines to check these:
    A) 4267 × 3899 = 16637033
    B) 816 × 5553 = 4531248
    C) 23 × 8670 = 199210

2. 3^4 = ? You won't need logs for this problem.

3. 4^3 = ?

4. A Rag-A-Fluffy doll weighs 765 grams. Its pacifier weighs one-third as much as the doll. How much does the pacifier weigh?

5. Find the next prime number after 29.

$\cdots\cdots$ANSWERS$\cdots\cdots$

1. A) $4267 \times 3899 = 16637033$

$4267 \twoheadrightarrow 4+2+6+7 = 19$ $19 \twoheadrightarrow 1+9 = 10$ $10 \twoheadrightarrow 1+0 = \underline{1}$

Similarly, $3899 \twoheadrightarrow \underline{2}$ and $16637033 \twoheadrightarrow \underline{2}$

Since $1 \times 2 = 2$, this multiplication checks.

   B) $816 \times 5553 = 4531248$

   $\twoheadrightarrow 6$ $\twoheadrightarrow 9$ $\twoheadrightarrow 9$ $6 \times 9 = 54 \twoheadrightarrow 5+4 = 9$

   This checks.

   C) $23 \times 8670 = 199210$

   $\twoheadrightarrow 5$ $\twoheadrightarrow 3$ $\twoheadrightarrow 4$ $5 \times 3 = 15 \twoheadrightarrow 1+5 = 6$

   This does not check.

2. $3^4 = 3 \times 3 \times 3 \times 3 = 9 \times 3 \times 3 = 27 \times 3 = 81$

3. $4^3 = 4 \times 4 \times 4 = 64$

4. We want one-third of 765 grams. If you don't know whether to add, subtract, multiply, or divide, restate the problem with easier numbers. One-third of 6 is 2. We divided by 3.

$$\begin{array}{r} 255 \\ 3\overline{)\ 765} \\ \underline{6} \\ 16 \\ \underline{15} \\ 15 \\ \underline{15} \end{array}$$

The pacifier
weighs 255 grams.

5. 30 won't work. It has 8 numbers that divide evenly into it: 1, 2, 3, 5, 6, 10, 15, 30.

   31 works. It is the next prime after 29.

Chapter Five
The Long View of Life

It was half past five. People were finishing up their pizzas and heading home. Many stopped and thanked Elaine Marie for presenting the best Math and Pizza Conference that they had ever attended.

When Darlene and Joe left, Joe was talking about getting an after-pizza snack.

Betty and Alexander headed back to their apartments. They each had reading to do for tomorrow's classes. Monday was coming quickly.

5:30

a pizza-making robot

Stanthony sent the 19 pizza-making robots back to their home. He had rented the robots for one hour and owed $114. He wrote out a check and gave it to one of the robots to carry back to Robot Rentals.

$$19\overline{)114} \quad \begin{array}{r} 6 \\ \underline{114} \end{array}$$

Each robot had cost $6.

Fred headed outside and began walking toward his office. After several blocks he entered the KITTENS campus. It was getting to be twilight, that time between when the sun sets and the darkness of night comes.

It was quiet. That felt good.

The hours at the conference had been busy and noisy. Those hours had also been good.

Fred thought, *Life needs both times: the active, loud times and the still, silent times.*

He just walked and let his mind settle down.

☞ He wasn't trying to figure out how to make Honey Cards.

☞ He wasn't planning an apiary.

☞ He wasn't shopping for an ice cream maker for 800 people.

☞ He wasn't desperately trying to think of a 17-letter plural word.

Fred was just being—not doing.

He briefly thought of Joe who starts his morning by turning on both the radio and the television, who spends his whole day talking and eating. Joe would never notice the stars unless one of them exploded. He would never notice a perfect rose unless it told him, "Eat me. I taste like chocolate." He never took the long view of life—to think about your whole life and what you want to do with it. In short, Joe was like a cow in the field that just does all the things that cows do without giving a thought about tomorrow.

Cows do not take
the long view of life.

When Joe falls asleep at night, it is often with the radio on and jelly beans in his mouth.*

Fred let go of thoughts of Joe. Rather than trying to actively solve something, he was being quiet and letting whatever was cooking in his mind drift to the surface. It was like dreaming while you are awake.

There are times in life to swim and times to float.

He sat under a big tree. He looked at his shoes. He thought of the nine times table and noticed that every answer added to nine.

$1 \times 9 = 9$	9
$2 \times 9 = 18$	$1 + 8 = 9$
$3 \times 9 = 27$	$2 + 7 = 9$
$4 \times 9 = 36$	$3 + 6 = 9$
$5 \times 9 = 45$	$4 + 5 = 9$
$6 \times 9 = 54$	$5 + 4 = 9$
$7 \times 9 = 63$	$6 + 3 = 9$
$8 \times 9 = 72$	$7 + 2 = 9$
$9 \times 9 = 81$	$8 + 1 = 9$

---

* A great way to rot your teeth!

He thought of Raggy and Kingie and wondered whether his children someday would play with dolls.

He had never met any girl that he wanted to marry but he was only five years old. There was still a little bit of time.

He thought about what it would be like to bring a flashlight and read a book under a tree at night.

He remembered books each of which he had read in a single afternoon. *The Wind in the Willows. The Old Man and the Sea.*

Multiplication and division are pairs. What would go with the union of two sets? {cat, dog} ∪ {dog, rat} = {cat, dog, rat}

It might be the **intersection** of two sets.

{cat, dog} ∩ {dog, rat} = {dog}

Union of two sets are those things that are in *either* set. ∪

Intersection of two sets are those things that are in *both* sets. ∩

{Kansas, ☺, ξ} ∩ {Nevada, ☻, canary} = {   }

{M, N, P, Q} ∩ {M, N, P, Q} = {M, N, P, Q}

Your Turn to Play

1. {horse, clock, razor, shoe} ∩ {storm, shoe} = ?

2. What is the next prime after 31?

3. Is this correct?

    $56{,}647 \times 7{,}686 \ = \ 435{,}358{,}842$

4. Is the intersection of two sets a commutative operation?

5. $5^3 = ?$

6. Write one billion as a numeral.

7. 6xyz + 9xyz = ?

Hard question

8. Suppose we have two sets. Call them A and B.
Suppose we know that A ∩ B = B.
What can we say about A and B?

Really hard question

9. We have two sets, A and B. Suppose we know that
A ∪ B = A ∩ B.
What can we say about A and B?

.... ANSWERS ....

1. {horse, clock, razor, shoe} ∩ {storm, shoe} = {shoe}

2. 32 won't work. It has 6 numbers that divide evenly into it: 1, 2, 4, 8, 16, 32.
   33 won't work. It has 4 numbers that divide evenly into it: 1, 3, 11, 33.
   34 won't work. It has 4 numbers that divide evenly into it: 1, 2, 17, 34.
   35 won't work. It has 4 numbers that divide evenly into it: 1, 5, 7, 35.
   36 won't work. It has 9 numbers that divide evenly into it: 1, 2, 3, 4, 6, 9, 12, 18, 36.

37 works. It is the next prime after 31.

3. Is this correct?

$$56{,}647 \times 7{,}686 = 435{,}358{,}842$$

⟫ 1   ⟫ 9   ⟫ 6 $1 \times 9 = 9$

                                            This does not check.

4. For any two sets, A and B, is it always true that A ∩ B gives the same answer as B ∩ A?

A ∩ B asks the question, "What are the elements that are in both A and B?"

B ∩ A asks the question, "What are the elements that are in both B and A?"

It is always true that A ∩ B equals B ∩ A.

Intersection is a commutative operation.

5. $5^3 = 5 \times 5 \times 5 = 25 \times 5 = 125$

6.
one thousand	1,000	10^3
one million	1,000,000	10^6
one billion	1,000,000,000	10^9
one trillion	1,000,000,000,000	10^{12}

Billions and trillions used to be called astronomical numbers since the only place that you encountered them was in astronomy. There can be billions of stars in a galaxy.

Nowadays, billions and trillions are most often mentioned in connection with government debt.

7. 6xyz + 9xyz = 15xyz

8. We are given A ∩ B = B.

If we look at an example:

{1, 2, 3, 4, 5, 6} ∩ {1, 2, 3, 4, 5} = {1, 2, 3, 4, 5}, we see that the only way that A ∩ B could equal B would be that every element of B was also in A.

(One reader in ten would have gotten this correct.)

9. We are given A ∪ B = A ∩ B.

A ∪ B means those things that are in either A or B.

A ∩ B means those things that are in both A and B.

A ∪ B is equal to A ∩ B implies that everything that is in either set, A ∪ B, must be in both sets, A ∩ B.

Then A and B must have the same members.

Everything that is in A must be in B.
Everything that is in B must be in A.

Therefore, A = B.

(One reader in a hundred would have gotten this question correct.)

Chapter Six
More Than White Dots

As Fred sat under a big tree on the KITTENS campus, he looked up at the Orion constellation.

Betelgeuse
"beatle juice"
a red super-giant
star

Orion Nebula
big cloud of glowing
dust and gas

When he was a baby and looked at the night sky, he thought that the stars were just holes in a big black cloth that let in the light. He thought that if you were really tall, you could reach up and touch those holes.

Now he knows that the middle "star" in Orion's sword isn't a star. Now he knows that astronomers estimate that sometime in the next million years Betelgeuse will become a super nova (really explode) and become brighter than the moon. Fred figured that he had about one chance in ten thousand of seeing that. (If you divide one hundred into one million, the quotient will be ten thousand.)

$$\text{divisor}\overline{)\,\text{dividend}}^{\text{quotient}}$$

(KWO-shent)

Fred was making a rough estimate. One million was an approximate number. One hundred was a very rough estimate of Fred's life span.

$$100\overline{)1000000}^{\,10000}$$
$$\underline{100}$$

❀ If you didn't know anything about astronomy, all you would see in the night sky would be white dots.

❀ If you didn't know anything about division, you couldn't figure out that you had one chance in 10,000 of seeing Betelgeuse explode.

❀ If you didn't have much of a vocabulary, you couldn't think very deeply. Example ⇨ TV good. Pizza good. Day good. Night tiger bad.

❀ When a doctor listens to your heart with a stethoscope, he/she will hear much more than you could hear. All you hear is thump-thump-thump.

WHAT YOU EXPERIENCE DEPENDS SO MUCH ON WHAT YOU KNOW.

That is why education is so important. The better your education, the more you can see.

Would you want a doctor who couldn't tell the difference between a fever and femur?*

Would you want an auto mechanic who confused cantaloupes with carburetors?**

Would you want a math teacher who couldn't tell the difference between a cardinal and a cardinal number?***

Red ↘

"Do I look like a cardinal number?"

If you show 7^2 to most four-year-olds, they will tell you, "You are a very poor writer. You are supposed to write your numbers all the same size."

They don't know that 7^2 means 7 × 7, which is 49.

---

* Femur = the thigh bone, the big bone between knee and hip.

** A carburetor mixes gasoline with air. The mixture of gasoline and air is then ignited by the spark plug. If you light gasoline, it burns. If you light a mixture of gasoline and air, it explodes.

*** Cardinal numbers are used to count the number of members of a set. The cardinal number associated with {♣,♦,♥,♠} is four.

Your Turn to Play

Suppose set A is the even natural numbers {2, 4, 6, 8, 10, 12, . . .}.

Suppose set B is the odd natural numbers {1, 3, 5, 7, 9, 11, 13, . . .}.

1. What is A ∪ B equal to?

2. What is A ∩ B equal to?

3. Numbers that end in 0, 2, 4, 6, or 8 are even numbers. Even numbers are all evenly divisible by two. Could 892,986,555,734 be a prime number?

4. 8^2 = ?

[A question for people who like English]

5. How good are you at proofreading? Excise (cut out) the word that doesn't belong: `This is a test to to see if you can do a good job of proofreading.`

[A question for art students]

6. Here are two famous heads. Draw what Fred would look like if he were a cardinal.

cardinal

.......ANSWERS.......

1. {2, 4, 6, 8, 10, 12, . . .} ∪ {1, 3, 5, 7, 9, 11, 13, . . .} is the set of all natural numbers that are either even or odd. That would equal all natural numbers.
A ∪ B = {1, 2, 3, 4, 5, . . .}.

2. {2, 4, 6, 8, 10, 12, . . .} ∩ {1, 3, 5, 7, 9, 11, 13, . . .} is the set of all natural numbers that are both even and odd at the same time. No natural number is both even and odd.

A ∩ B = {   }, which is known as the empty set.

3. 892,986,555,734 can't be a prime number because it has at least three divisors, namely 1, 2, and 892,986,555,734.

4. $8^2 = 8 \times 8 = 64$

5. The sentence has the word *to* twice.

6. Here are my attempts at drawing Fred if he were a cardinal. Your drawing will probably be better than mine.

Chapter Seven
What to Do

Fred felt a little chill. It was 6 p.m. Sitting under a big tree on the KITTENS campus wasn't the warmest place to be.* He wondered what to do with himself until bedtime.

✓ He had already gone jogging this morning.

✓ He had all his lectures ready for Monday, so he didn't need to work in his office (assuming classes weren't canceled).

✓ He wasn't hungry. (Some people eat just because they are bored.)

✓ The KITTENS University library closed at 5 p.m. on Sundays.

✓ The King KITTENS shopping mall was open but there was nothing that Fred needed to buy. (Some people shop because they are bored.)

✓ He didn't own a television set.

✓ His office was very neat, so he didn't have to clean it up.

---

* Another example of litotes. (LIE-toe-tease) Litotes is saying the opposite of what you mean and putting a *not* in front.

Fred is not extremely tall.	He is short.
Shoes do not taste very good.	Shoes taste terrible.
Joe doesn't hate fishing.	Joe loves fishing.

Fred wondered what was happening on campus tonight. Universities often offer special events: art receptions, symphonies, lectures, plays, planetarium shows, conferences, and, of course, sports.

Fred stood up and walked to the newspaper stand. The campus newspaper would tell him what was happening tonight.

THE KITTEN Caboodle

The Official Campus Newspaper of KITTENS University   Sunday 5:55 p.m.   10¢

Prisoners Escape!

KANSAS: C. C. Coalback and his sister escaped from the county jail at four o'clock this afternoon.

This is the second time they have escaped in the last two days.

Everyone in the KITTENS campus area is asked to be on the lookout for them.

University president declared this evening that escaped prisoners should not come on campus.

"I'm making that a rule," he said.

How that would be enforced was not clear.

The police chief said, "I think we are going to have to change our jail policy. Two years ago the Convicts' Rights Are Paramount group told us that we couldn't lock the jail doors because that made the prisoners uncomfortable. I think we are going to have to start locking the doors."

Fred heard a cough.

"Excuse me, honey," she said. "Do you have a cigarette. I haven't had a smoke all day, and I'm dying for one."

Fred recognized her immediately even though he couldn't see her that well since it was dark. Two things gave her away: her cough and her smell.

ashtray mouth

Fred didn't stand there and explain that he wasn't carrying cigarettes. He ran.

small essay

Avoiding Evil

When confronted with bad things (temptations, thieves, dragons,* monsters,* griffins,* people with knives) often the best thing to do is to look down and locate your legs . . . and use them! Walk or run.

end of small essay

He had run three steps, and someone grabbed him by the back of his shirt and lifted him off the ground. Fred's legs were still running but he wasn't going anywhere.

C. C. Coalback took Fred's seven Pizza Buttons and his eight

---

* These do not exist. They are imaginary.

Brass Braces and the three cents that Fred had.

Fred had spent most of the $400 honorarium that he had received.

ice cream maker	150.00
recipe book	6.00
milk, sugar, vanilla	242.70
7 Pizza Buttons (@ 9¢ each) @ = "at"	0.63
8 Brass Braces (@ 8¢ each)	0.64
	$399.97

He had started with $400.00
He spent   − $399.97
He had left $ 0.03

THREE THINGS TO KNOW

1. $892.37 means eight hundred ninety-two dollars and thirty-seven cents.

2. $892.37

   ↑ This dot is called a **decimal point**.

3. When you add numbers with decimal points in them, you just line up the decimal points and add.

$$
\begin{array}{r}
2.43 \\
15.04 \\
+\ \ 7.22 \\
\hline
24.69
\end{array}
$$

FIVE KINDS OF ●

| This is a sentence.

Period | 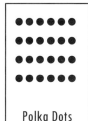

Polka Dots | Random Dots | $58.08

Decimal Point | 

Freckles |

Your Turn to Play

1. If Joe bought 8 jelly beans (@ 3¢ each) and paid a dollar, count back the change.

2. If Darlene bought 6 curlers (@ 7¢ each) and paid a dollar, count back the change.

When you count back change, you start with pennies, then nickels, then dimes, then quarters.

In contrast, when you want to pay a particular amount of money, say **43¢**, you work in the opposite direction. You start with quarters, then dimes, then nickels, then pennies.

To count out 43¢: **25 → 35 → 40 → 41 → 42 → 43**

3. Count out 55¢.

4. Count out 23¢.

5. Count out 38¢.

6. {#, &, @} ∩ {3, #, 887}

7. Is this correct? $4{,}673 \times 55{,}578 = 259{,}715{,}994$

. . . . **ANSWERS** . . . .

1. Eight jelly beans @ 3¢ each equals 24¢.
Counting back the change:
    24 → 25 → 50 → 75 → one dollar.

2. Six curlers @ 7¢ each equals 42¢.
Counting back the change:
    42 → 43 → 44 → 45 → 50 → 75 → one dollar.

3. To count out 55¢:
    25 → 50 → 55.

4. To count out 23¢:
    10 → 20 → 21 → 22 → 23.

5. To count out 38¢:
    25 → 35 → 36 → 37 → 38.

6. {#, &, @} ∩ {3, #, 887} = {#}

7. Using casting out nines:

    4,673 × 55,578 = 259,715,994

     ⇛ 2   ⇛ 3   ⇛ 6   2 × 3 = 6 It checks.

Chapter Eight
Sunday Evening

Coalback dropped Fred after taking his Pizza Buttons, his Brass Braces, and his three cents. Fred ran away.

Coalback didn't share any of the things he had stolen from Fred with his sister.

Fred ran to the police station on the campus. Only one small office in the back of the building was used since there was only one police officer for KITTENS University. The rest of the building was vacant. The billion dollars (10^9) that the federal government had spent to construct this edifice was wasted money.

The Millard Fillmore Police Station

On the front door was a sign. This was Sunday evening. Fred didn't know what to do.

Hours
M–F 9–3
closed weekends

He spotted Joe and Darlene. Joe was carrying a large bag of Jelly Stomach Jelly Beans. This was his after-pizza snack that Darlene had bought for him.

"Do either of you have a cell phone?" Fred asked. "I just saw Coalback and his sister. They have escaped from jail, and I need to report them."

Darlene pulled her cell phone out of her purse and offered it to Fred. Joe had never figured out why someone would have a cell phone in the shape of a wedding cake.

Darlene's wedding cake cell phone

Joe's phone was in the shape of one of his favorite foods: a jelly bean.

Jelly bean cell phone

Fred selected Joe's phone. It looked like it would be much easier to use. He called the county jail and said that he had just seen the escaped prisoners. Fred was so excited that he forgot to mention where he had seen them.

Fred handed the phone back to Joe. A second later his phone rang.

Joe answered, listened for a moment, and said, "No." He put his phone back in his pocket.

Darlene asked Joe, "What was that all about?"

Joe shrugged his shoulders and said, "It was the county jail. They asked if I had just called them about some escaped prisoners."

Joe and Darlene headed off to watch some television. There was a program they didn't want to miss: Roller Derby Reruns.

Coalback and his sister knew that they needed a place to stay, a place where no one would spot them. He knew the perfect spot. They broke into the Millard Fillmore Police Station and took up residence in two rooms on the third floor of the building. They would live there for years and no one would ever notice.

Fred was alone. He turned to the second page of the school newspaper for some ideas.

THE KITTEN Caboodle

The Official Campus Newspaper of KITTENS University   Page Two

Tonight's Events:

7 p.m. All-you-can-eat Spaghetti at Stanthony's PieOne.

7 p.m. Welcome-back parade, reception, and ball for our returning university president.

7 p.m. Debate Club. Tonight's topic: "Should Egg Rolls Be Buttered?"

| **Weather Report** |
| Tonight: Increasing darkness. |

7 p.m. Wrestling Club meets.

7 p.m. Would you like to be an actor? Open Auditions! The Drama Club will be performing Shakespeare's *A Midsummer Night's Dream* in March. Come and see what part you will play. We have a special need for short actors. We'll meet in room 100 of the Math Building.

The words *a special need for short actors* caught Fred's attention.

Ever since Fred had seen the movie *Pinocchio* and heard the song "Hi-Diddle-Dee-Dee, An Actor's Life for Me," he wondered what it would be like to be an actor. Now was his chance.

And they are meeting in the same building as my office is in, Fred thought. *This is perfect.* He ran across campus to the Math Building and climbed two flights of stairs up to his office.

Kingie was just finishing an oil painting when Fred rushed into the office.

"I'm going to be an actor!" Fred exclaimed. "They are doing *A Midsummer Night's Dream* and I hope they pick me to play the part of Robin Goodfellow, the Puck."

"Autumn Pond"
by Kingie

puck ⟶

The only puck that Kingie knew about was in ice hockey.

Fred had read all the plays of Shakespeare, and knew that Puck was a little guy that does a lot of high-spirited things in *A Midsummer Night's Dream*. Playing the part of Puck would be a lot of fun.

Your Turn to Play

1. Joe's large bag of Jelly Stomach Jelly Beans contained 7,317 beans. (Joe had counted them.) There are 271 beans in each pound. How many pounds did Joe's jelly beans weigh?

2. If the sum of the digits of a number are divisible by three, then the number is divisible by three.

    For example, 264 ⇛ 2 + 6 + 4 = 12. Since 12 is divisible evenly by 3, so is 264.

    With that in mind, find the next prime after 37.

3. Find the values of x, y, and z:
$$10^x = 1,000$$
$$10^y = 1,000,000$$
$$10^z = \text{one billion}$$

4. $\sum\limits_{i=3}^{5} iy = ?$

    (Sigma notation was done on pages 23, 24, 30, 47, and 53 of *Life of Fred: Ice Cream*.)

. . . . **ANSWERS** . . . .

1. There are 7,317 beans. There are 271 beans in each
pound. If you don't know whether to add, subtract, multiply, or divide, restate the
problem using smaller numbers. Suppose there were 12 beans and 3 beans in each pound.
Then the bag would weigh 4 pounds. We divided.

$$
\begin{array}{r}
27 \\
271\overline{)7317} \\
\underline{542} \\
1897 \\
\underline{1897}
\end{array}
$$

The bag weighs 27 lbs.

2. Finding the next prime after 37 . . .

It won't be 38 since 38 is even. 1, 2, and 38 divide evenly into 38.

It won't be 39 since 3 divides evenly into 39 (the sum of the digits of 39 is 12, which can be
divided by 3). 1, 3, and 39 divide evenly into 39.

It won't be 40 since 40 is even. 1, 2, and 40 divide evenly into 40.

41 works. The only two divisors of 41 are 1 and 41.

3. $10^3 = 1{,}000$ since $10 \times 10 \times 10 = 1{,}000$

$10^6 = 1{,}000{,}000$

$10^9 = $ one billion $= 1{,}000{,}000{,}000$

In Advanced Algebra, we will learn about logs. If
you have a scientific calculator (one that has keys
marked sin, cos, log), you can find out a little about logs.
Type in 1000 and hit the log key. The answer will be 3.

4. $\displaystyle\sum_{i=3}^{5} iy = 3y + 4y + 5y = 12y$

Chapter Nine
Packing for the Audition

Fred had never been to an audition. All he knew was that they were going to pick people to play each of the parts. Fred had seen *A Midsummer Night's Dream*, and he knew that Puck ran around and did a lot of giggling.

Fred practiced that in his office. Kingie thought Fred was going nuts.

In one performance of the play that Fred had seen, Puck looked like:

In another performance, he looked like:

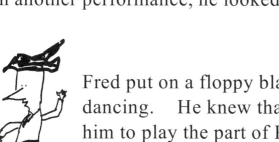

Fred put on a floppy black hat and practiced dancing. He knew that they would choose him to play the part of Robin Goodfellow, the Puck.

He didn't know what to bring to an audition. He selected three hats (the black one, a green one for scenes in the forest, and a blue one to match the sky). He had five shirts (red for comedy, black for night scenes, blue for sad scenes, pink for giggling, and polka dot for luck).

He picked three pair of shoes (ballet for dancing on his toes, tap shoes, and cleats in case he had to run in the mud).

He then had 45 possible combinations (3 × 5 × 3) that he could wear.

He found an empty box and wrote his name on the outside. The box was 12 inches wide, 16 inches long and 10 inches tall.

In algebra the formula for the volume of a box is V = *lwh* where *l* is the length, *w* is the width, and *h* is the height.

Fred's box had a volume of 16 × 12 × 10 which is 1,920 cubic inches.

He put the hats, shirts, and shoes in the box. There was still room left, so he tossed in a clipboard and some pens in case he needed to take notes. *The director may give me some special acting instructions,* Fred thought.

6:45 p.m.

It was a quarter to seven. Fred had 15 minutes before the audition. Fred pulled his Shakespeare book off the shelf and turned to *A Midsummer Night's Dream.* He had read the play before and wanted to refresh his memory in case the director quizzed him about the plot.

Fred wrote an outline of the plot: Theseus and Hippolyta
were going to get married at the next new moon.[*] Everybody is supposed to
get ready to celebrate. Two young men: Lysander and Demetrius. Two young
women: Hermia and Helena.

Lysander loves Hermia. Demetrius loves Hermia more than Helena.
Hermia loves Lysander more than Demetrius. Helena loves Demetrius. And
Hermia's dad wants her to marry Demetrius.

Fairies meet in the woods. They have also come to celebrate the
wedding. The king and queen of the fairies have a quarrel. The king sends
his jester, whose name is Puck, to magically change who loves whom.
Lysander starts loving Helena more than Hermia. The queen falls in love with
a weaver (who has been turned into a donkey). Demetrius starts loving
Helena more than Hermia. All the young men and women are quarreling but
the queen is super happy with her donkey.

That's as far as Fred could get. He had
done the first three (out of five) acts. It was
getting near 7 p.m. so Fred picked up his box
and headed down the stairs to the audition room
on the first floor.

Time Out!

While Fred is heading down to
room 100, it should be noted that
Fred's notes left out a lot of the
action of the play.

In the first act, a bunch of craftsmen (a carpenter,
a weaver, a bellows-mender, a joiner, a tailor, and a
tinker) get together to rehearse a play that they are

---

[*] A new moon is the opposite of a full moon. A new moon could be called "a no
moon."

going to put on to celebrate the wedding. Puck changes the weaver into a donkey and all the other craftsmen are frightened and run away.

The queen, who has fallen in love with the donkey, has all her little fairies wait on the donkey. It's all very cute.

As you might have noticed, this is all much more complicated than figuring out that $16 \times 12 \times 10$ equals 1,920.

English major or math major—it's your choice. If you like complicated plots, enjoy watching little fairies wait on a donkey, and writing long term papers, then be an English major.

Math majors enjoy: (1) much less to read, (2) much less to memorize, (3) no silly spelling rules (*bot* is spelled *bought*, and *yought* is spelled *yacht*), (4) no donkeys, and (5) probably better job opportunities and better pay.

What math book ever mentions donkeys?

On the way down the stairs, Fred wondered whether he should have written up a résumé (RES-zoo-may). Résumés are often required for job interviews. They list the personal, educational, and professional qualifications and experience that a job applicant has.

Fred imagined that there would be hundreds of people showing up for the audition.

Your Turn to Play

1. We read, "Fred's box had a volume of $16 \times 12 \times 10$ which is 1,920 cubic inches." Show that that is true.

2. Fred's empty box weighed 1 lb. 9 oz. The hats he put into the box weighed a total of 3 lbs. 2 oz. The shirts weighed a total of 4 lbs. 5 oz. The shoes, 5 lbs. 4 oz. The clipboard and pens weighed 1 lb.

How much did the whole thing weigh?   (One pound = 16 ounces.)

3. Is 2,000,000,005,000 a prime number?

4. Is 2,000,000,000,001 a prime number?

5. Find the value of x so that $x^2 = 100$

[Question for art students]

6. If Fred were auditioning for the part of Pinocchio, he would have to have a nose that could grow much longer whenever he told a lie. What would Fred look like with a longer nose?

[Hard question for students who love logic]

7. Suppose Fred were playing Pinocchio. His nose would only grow really long if he said something that was untrue.

Suppose Fred said, "My nose will grow longer right now." What would happen?

········ANSWERS········

1. Here's the work:

$$
\begin{array}{r}
16 \\
\times\ 12 \\
\hline
32 \\
16 \\
\hline
192
\end{array}
$$

and then $192 \times 10 = 1{,}920.$

2.

1 lb.	9 oz.
3 lbs.	2 oz.
4 lbs.	5 oz.
5 lbs.	4 oz.
1 lb.	

14 lbs.   20 oz.   and since 20 oz. = 1 lb. 4 oz. the final answer is 15 lbs. 4 oz.

3. 2,000,000,005,000 is a even number. So it is divisible by 1, 2, and 2,000,000,005,000. It is not prime.

4. The sum of the digits of 2,000,000,000,001 is 3, which is evenly divisible by 3. Therefore, 2,000,000,000,001 is evenly divisible by 3. (We learned this in the previous Your Turn to Play.)
So 2,000,000,000,001 is divisible by 1, 3, and 2,000,000,000,001. It is not a prime.

5. $10^2 = 100$ so x = 10.

6. Here is my drawing. ─────────────

7. If it grew longer, then Fred was telling the truth, and it wouldn't have grown longer.

If it didn't grow longer, then Fred wasn't telling the truth and it would have grown longer.

This is called a **paradox**. (PAIR-o-docks)

Chapter Ten
The Director

There were three students standing outside room 100—two boys and a girl. Fred thought that they were there to help with crowd control. He imagined that there were hundreds of students packed into the room.

"Is there any more space inside the room?" Fred asked. "Am I too late?"

"Hi, Professor Gauss," the three students all said. They were all his students.

One of them asked, "Do you have a key to this room. It's locked, and we can't get in."

It slowly dawned on Fred that only four people had shown up for the audition.

The director showed up and unlocked the door. Everyone went inside.

Famous director William Manage

The director began, "Good evening lady and gentlemen and boy. In three weeks, we will present *A Midsummer Night's Dream*."

Fred was so pleased. Mr. Manage was a very famous director who was known for putting on plays under impossible situations. Everyone liked

to work for him. He was always optimistic.
(Optimist = a person who looks on the bright
side of things, who has positive thoughts.)

One of the boys raised his hand and said,
"The play has a lot of parts,*but there are only
four of us."

The director smiled. "That's no problem.
Some of you may get to play more than one part,
and I, as director, can always rewrite the play.
We'll manage."

The girl raised her hand, "Putting on a play
of Shakespeare's usually takes months of
preparation. Last year I played Juliet in *Romeo
and Juliet,* and we spent three months
rehearsing, making the costumes and the sets.
Did you say three weeks?"

"That's not a problem. The last five plays
that I have directed have taken an average of
three weeks to prepare. *Hamlet* took 2 weeks;
The Merchant of Venice took 1 week; *Macbeth*
took 2 weeks; *Julius Caesar* took 1 week; *King
Lear* took 9 weeks. *King Lear* took longer
because we had trouble with the scene where

---

* Theseus and Hippolyta (who are getting married), the two young men (Lysander and
Demetrius), the two young women (Hermia and Helena), Philostrate (the one who will
be in charge of the wedding celebration), the carpenter, the weaver, the bellows-
mender, the joiner (a carpenter who specializes in making doors, windows, and
panels), a tailor, a tinker (one who mends pots and pans), the king and queen of the
fairies, and four fairies.

Lear wanders in the storm. It was hard to make it rain on stage. But don't worry. We can do *Dream* in three weeks. We'll manage."

Fred heard numbers and his mind went into high gear. He thought, *the median average of 1, 1, 2, 2, and 9 is 2. That's the number in the middle when you line up the numbers from smallest to largest.**

*Maybe Mr. Manage is using the **mean average**. You add up all the numbers and divide by the number of numbers. We add up the five numbers—1 + 1 + 2 + 2 + 9—and get 15, and then divide by 5. 15 ÷ 5 is 3. Yes. He was using the mean average.*

"We begin working tonight," Will Manage announced. "There's not a moment to lose. We have three weeks. There are 24 hours in a day. You may spend 4 of them sleeping. That leaves 20 hours each day to work on the play."

"But what about my being a student?" one of the boys asked. Fred mentally added, *And my being a teacher?*

"Nothing to worry about. You may have read that tonight the university president is being welcomed back from his vacation. By

---

* Median averages were done in *Life of Fred: Farming.*

tomorrow, he will be off on his usual three-week spring vacation in Las Vegas. He is certain to cancel classes again."

Fred was already starting to feel tired thinking about surviving on four hours of sleep each night. Young kids need more sleep than old people.

Many directors talk a lot. This director was no exception. "Let's start by assigning roles."

He pointed to one of the boys and said, "You will be the king of the fairies."

"And you," pointing to the girl, "will be the queen."

"And you," pointing to Fred, "will be all four fairies rolled into one part."

Selecting who would play the two young men, Lysander and Demetrius, was easy.

Helena is a tall blond in the play. The director selected the girl to play Helena.

Hermia is a short brunette. There was only one possibility. Fred would have to play Hermia. Fred would be supplied with a dark brown wig. The director explained to Fred that he didn't have to be embarrassed. In Shakespeare's time (around 1600) every part was played by men or boys.

"Why was that?" the girl asked.

The director shrugged his shoulders and said, "It seems that every generation does things that seem totally stupid thirty years later.

"For example, on March 3, 1939, a Harvard freshman ate a three-inch live goldfish. On March 26, a sophomore ate 23 live goldfish. When a student at Kutztown State University ate 43 of them, he was suspended from school for 'conduct unbecoming to a student.'

"A student at St. Mary's University ate 210 live goldfish. The whole fad lasted about two months.

"Newspapers spent a lot of space reporting this stupidity—space they might have used to describe the situation in Europe. World War II was about to begin later that year."

Your Turn to Play

1. Find the median average of 44, 2, and 56.

2. Find the mean average of 44, 2, and 56.

3. If there are, say, 20 parts in the play and they are assigned equally to 4 actors, how many parts would each actor get to play?

4. $\sum_{i=7}^{9} 6i = ?$

. . . . ANSWERS . . . .

1. To find the median average of 44, 2, and 56, you first arrange the numbers from smallest to largest:

2, 44, 56

and then you pick the number in the middle. The median average is 44.

2. To find the mean average of 44, 2, and 56, you add up the three numbers—44 + 2 + 56 = 102—and then divide by the number of addends.*

The mean average
is 34.

$$\begin{array}{r} 34 \\ 3\overline{)102} \\ \underline{9} \\ 12 \\ \underline{12} \end{array}$$

3. **Twenty parts and 4 actors.** If you are not sure whether to add, subtract, multiply, or divide, restate the problem with easier numbers. Suppose there are 6 parts and 2 actors. Then each actor would play 3 parts. You divided.

$$4\overline{)20} \quad \begin{array}{c} 5 \end{array}$$ Each actor would play five parts.

4. $\sum\limits_{i=7}^{9} 6i = 6(7) + 6(8) + 6(9)$

$$\begin{array}{r} 42 \\ 48 \\ + \ 54 \\ \hline 144 \end{array}$$

6(7) means 6 × 7.

This could also be written as (6)(7) or (6)7 or 6·7.

6·7 is not very often used because it can be confused with a decimal point: 6.7.

---

* Addends are numbers that you add together. Here are four addends: 7 + 3 + 5 + 2.

Chapter Eleven
Costumes

The director continued to assign parts to the four actors. Instead of having six craftsmen, there will be only four of them. The girl will play the part of the bellows-mender. One of the boys will be the weaver who gets turned into the donkey.

Fred was holding his breath. There was one part that he really wanted to play.

Finally, the director announced, "And, of course, you," pointing to Fred, "will play the part of Puck."

Now, the thought of working on the play 20 hours each day didn't seem so bad.

The director handed each actor a copy of the play. It was time for the first reading. Each person read their part aloud so that everyone could get a sense of the whole play and their role in it.

Puck (Fred) had the last 16 lines of the play in which he expressed the hope that the play had offended no one.

After assigning the parts and the initial read through, the next thing was making the costumes. They all headed to the wardrobe room in the Drama Building.

It was already twenty-five minutes after eight. It was getting close to Fred's bedtime.

8:25 p.m.

It was only a five-minute walk. They were in the wardrobe room by half past eight.

The wardrobe room was huge. On one rack there were hundreds of different shirts.

There were thousands of hats. Fred liked to play with hats. After a minute of looking, he chose

The director suggested ———

Fred tried it on. His head was too small, or, as he preferred to express it, the hat was too large.

The director knew all the tricks. He wadded up some newspaper and stuffed it into the hat. Now it was perfect.

Picking out a shirt was easy. There was only one shirt that was small enough for Fred. When he tried it on, one of the buttons fell off. Fred panicked. He didn't know what to do. When you are five years old, there are many things in life that you have never experienced.*

He thought about gluing the button back on. The drawback: It wouldn't work.

He thought about just putting on the shirt and stapling it closed. The drawback: He would have to wear that shirt for the next three weeks.

He thought about running back to his office and getting one of his own shirts. The drawback: Almost all of Fred's shirts have ducks or bunnies on them. Those shirts were okay for teaching but not for playing the part of Puck.

He thought about crying but he was afraid that the director would throw him out of the play. He didn't realize that everybody cries. It's just what you cry about that changes as you grow older.

"Professor," one of the boys said, "Do you need help with that button? These costumes are so old. Some of them must have been here since the university was founded."

---

* And when you are 25, there are many things that you have not experienced. And when you are 35, 45, or 55, new situations still keep popping up.

Fred offered him the shirt and the button. He watched very closely as the boy threaded a needle and knotted the end of the thread.

There are about 50 basic survival skills that kids learn before they leave home. Since Fred had left home at the age of six months, he had never learned any of them. The first time that he tried to wash his clothes in the washing machine he put in a whole box of laundry detergent.

The boy sewed on the button and gave the shirt back to Fred.

Fred noticed that he had two pieces of his costumes done in 45 minutes. An ordered pair: (2, 45). When he started, he had none: (0, 0). He would be playing the parts of Puck, the four fairies, and Hermia. He would need a total of 16 costume pieces.

He plotted (0, 0) and (2, 45).

Then he drew a line through those two points.

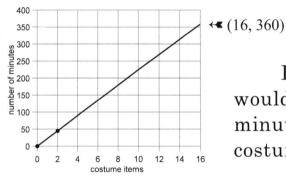

◂◀ (16, 360)

It looked like he would need about 360 minutes to gather 16 costume items.

The 360 minutes was just a rough estimate of how long it would take to get the 16 costume pieces ready. When he looked at his graph, he was guessing that the point was (16, 360) but it might have been (16, 365) or (16, 362).

The whole idea was to get a rough idea how long it would take. The play was going to be presented in three weeks. He needed to know if it would take six months to get his costumes ready.

Your Turn to Play

1. Convert 360 minutes into hours.

2. It was 8:30 p.m. when Fred started working on his costumes. If he did all that work tonight, when would he finish? ("All that work" is the hours in problem 1.)

3. Happily, he didn't have to do it all in one night. He had three weeks to get his costumes ready. How many days are in three weeks?

4. The spool of thread that the boy used to sew Fred's button on had 50 yards of thread. He used 7 inches. How much was left on the spool? (1 yard = 36 inches)

5. 7^3 = ?

(The 3 is called the **exponent**. We will use a lot of exponents in algebra.)

6. x^3 means xxx. What does x^5 mean?

7. [Harder question]. When you multiply x^3 times x^5, what is the answer? $(x^3)(x^5)$ = ?

(Hint: It is not x^{15}.)

. . . . **ANSWERS** . . . .

1. There are 60 minutes in an hour. We want to convert 360 minutes into hours. Restating the problem with easier numbers, suppose there are 5 minutes in an hour and we want to convert 10 minutes into hours. That would be 2 hours. We divided.

So in the original problem, we divide

$$60)\overline{360} \quad \begin{array}{r} 6 \\ \hline 360 \\ \hline \end{array}$$

360 minutes = 6 hours

2. We want 6 hours later than 8:30 p.m. Adding 4 hours to 8:30 p.m. takes us to 12:30 a.m. Then 2 more hours takes us to 2:30 a.m.

3. There are seven days in a week. Three weeks equals 21 days.

4.   50 yards

   −   7 inches
   ───────────────────

$$\begin{array}{lll} & \overset{49}{\cancel{50}} \text{ yards} & 36 \text{ inches} \\ - & & 7 \text{ inches} \\ \hline & 49 \text{ yards} & 29 \text{ inches} \end{array}$$

5. $7^3 = 7 \times 7 \times 7 = 49 \times 7$

$$\begin{array}{r} 49 \\ \times\ 7 \\ \hline 343 \end{array}$$

6. x^5 = xxxxx

7. $(x^3)(x^5)$ = (xxx)(xxxxx) = xxxxxxxx = x^8

So $x^3 x^5 = x^8$.

   This is one of the weird things you will learn in algebra.

Chapter Twelve
$4 - 1 - 1 = 2$

Fred found the box with all the wigs. He needed a wig to play the part of Hermia. Fred is five, so he had a lot of fun trying on every wig in the box.

One of the boys, the one who hadn't helped Fred with his button, had been sitting alone in a corner. He hadn't been trying on costumes. He stood up and walked over to the director.

"This isn't for me," he began. "And I can't see the four of us acting all those parts. And you tell us that classes will be canceled for the next three weeks. And when everyone else is off on vacation, we are supposed to be working 20 hours a day getting ready to present a play when they come back. And good luck to you guys." He walked out.

The director looked at the three remaining actors and said, "That's okay. I'm glad that he quit now rather than a week from now. I'll just rewrite the play a little and remove the part of Lysander and one of the craftsmen. It's no problem. We'll manage."

Fred thought this was going to be very exciting. For most of the play, either two or three actors would be on stage. There would be lots of quick costume changes.

The director continued, "In the fifth act, the six craftsmen are supposed to put on a play for the entertainment of Theseus and Hippolyta (who are getting married), the two young men (Lysander and Demetrius), the two young women (Hermia and Helena), and Philostrate who is in charge of the wedding celebration. Since there are now three craftsmen, there would be no one in the audience for that play. We will just have to omit the fifth act."

Fred hoped that the 16 lines that Puck says at the end of the fifth act would be transferred to the end of the fourth act. Since they were cutting out the fifth act, Puck's hope that the play had offended no one would be especially important.

The director sat down and started crossing off scenes out of the play.

He mumbled to himself, "If the craftsmen aren't presenting the play in the fifth act, then there is no need for them to rehearse the play in the third act."

This reminded Fred of **set subtraction**.

The director had taken the whole play and removed part of Act III and all of Act V. (In Roman numerals, III = 3 and V = 5.)

Fred did a bunch of set subtraction problems:

{4, 5, 87} – {4} = {5, 87}

{3, 9, 44} – {6, 8, 10} = {3, 9, 44}

{6, 202, 500} – {6, 202, 500} = {   }

{1, 2, 3, 4} – {4, 5, 6, 7} = {1, 2, 3}

If A and B are sets, then A – B is the set of all elements in A that are not in B.

Fred rewrote that definition: If something is in A – B, then two things must be true:

i) It must be in A, and

ii) It can not be in B.

The director announced, "We need to start building the sets." He meant the construction used for the backdrop of the play.

Fred thought he meant "a collection of things," which is what sets are in math. {north, Donald Duck, ℜ, Tennessee, ♪, ⚃, ℵ, KITTENS University, 555554, the ruby slippers, Monday} is an example a of set.* Sets can be *any* collection.

----

* My dictionary lists 87 different meanings for the word *set*. Setting your hair (using curlers to make it wavy) is different than setting a flag pole in concrete is different than setting plates on a table is different than setting the hands of a clock is different than setting a broken bone is different than. . . . It is amazing that we understand each other when we speak English.

"Much of *A Midsummer Night's Dream* happens in the forest," the director explained. "We want to build a really big forest. Then the audience won't notice that we have only three actors in the play."

Everyone moved to the set construction room. There were sheets of plywood that were four feet by eight feet. They nailed 15 sheets together to make a giant backdrop.

It was time to paint a forest on the backdrop. Fred painted the bottom part of the backdrop. The girl could reach up to the top of the first row of plywood. The boy got on a tall ladder and started painting the top section.

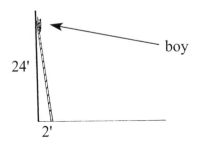

Fred computed the slope of that ladder. Slope is equal to $\frac{\text{Rise}}{\text{Run}}$ which is $24 \div 2 = 12$.

Ladders shouldn't have a slope of 12. Here is what might happen.

And that is exactly what did happen.

Your Turn to Play

1. Looking at the backdrop on the previous page, determine how wide it was.

2. Since the actors would have to paint that backdrop, it was important to know what the area was. What was the area?

[Question for creative readers]

3. Fred thought of a set in which all of the elements were different from each other. {north, Donald Duck, ℜ, Tennessee, ♪, ⠒, ℵ, KITTENS University, 555554, the ruby slippers, Monday}

Name a set with four elements in which all the elements are different from each other. Don't use any elements like those from Fred's set. Don't write {south, Daisy Duck, . . . }.

4. We now have three ways to combine sets.

$\{4, 5, 6\} \cup \{5, 6, 7\} = ?$

$\{4, 5, 6\} \cap \{5, 6, 7\} = ?$

$\{4, 5, 6\} - \{5, 6, 7\} = ?$

5. How many different ways do we have to combine numbers?

6. Two people were putting up a total of $8,000 to put on this play. Each contributed a half. How much did each contribute?

.... ANSWERS ....

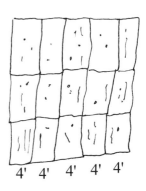

4' 4'   4'   4'   4'

1. Five times four feet is 20'.

2. The area of a rectangle is length times width. A = ℓ𝓌.

A = 24 × 20

```
      24
    × 20
    ----
      00
     48
    ----
     480
```
The area is 480 square feet.

3. Your set might have included a color, a fruit, a title of a book, the name of a movie star, the name of a star in the sky, the name of a brand of car, a gas such as hydrogen or helium, an article of clothing, a farm animal, a knot such as a square knot, your grandfather, a spice, a tool such as a hammer, or pizza.

4.   {4, 5, 6} ∪ {5, 6, 7} = {4, 5, 6, 7}

        {4, 5, 6} ∩ {5, 6, 7} = {5, 6}

        {4, 5, 6} − {5, 6, 7} = {4}

5. Let's take the numbers 4 and 5. Here are the ways I could think of: $4 + 5$ (addition), $4 − 5$ (subtraction), $4 × 5$ (multiplication), $4 ÷ 5$ (division), 4^5 (exponentiation), 45 (concatenation, which means sticking them together). You may not have thought of these last two examples.

6. Half of $8,000

```
      4000
    2) 8000
```

They each contributed $4,000.

Chapter Thirteen
William Butler Yeats

Most people, if they were called upon to direct *A Midsummer Night's Dream* with only two actors, might be discouraged.

William Manage was not like most people. He remembered what Winston Churchill said during World War II.*

Fred wondered what William was going to do. *Was the director going to cut more scenes out of the play until it became* A Midsummer Afternoon's Dream?

William told the girl and Fred, "We are going to make a quick switch. We are going to do *Romeo and Juliet* instead."

"Do you expect me to . . . Him, Romeo? You gotta be kidding. No way. I'm outta here."

Fred was relieved. He wanted to be an actor but he didn't want to do any of that romantic kissing stuff.

---

* "Never give in. Never give in. Never, never, never, never—in nothing, great or small, large or petty—never give in, except to convictions of honor and good sense."

William looked at Fred. Fred looked at William. Fred was expecting him to say, "We'll manage." He didn't.

William remembered the last part of what Churchill had said, ". . . never give in, except to convictions of honor and **good sense**."

He shook his head and recited to himself one of the most famous lines from the poet Yates, "Things fall apart; the center cannot hold."* There was a tear in his eye.

He turned to Fred and said, "I hear that there's an all-you-can-eat spaghetti feed at PieOne tonight. Would you care to join me?"

"No thank you. I think it's time I head home."

They turned off all the lights and headed out into the cold February air. William walked toward PieOne, and Fred toward the Math Building.

It was five minutes to nine. Fred's acting career had begun at 7. He had been an actor for one hour and fifty-five minutes.

8:55 p.m.

---

* Yates wrote this in 1919, the year after the end of the first World War. The next
lines are: Mere anarchy is loosed upon the world.
                The blood-dimmed tide is loosed, and everywhere
                The ceremony of innocence is drowned;
                The best lack all conviction, while the worst
                Are full of passionate intensity.

Fred thought about how bad the director must be feeling. For Fred it had only been a couple of hours that were lost. For the director, this was a failure in the main calling of his life.

Then he thought about the boy who had fallen off the ladder. He had been knocked unconscious and had been taken to the hospital. Fred changed direction and walked toward the hospital.

small essay

The Spring of Selfishness

Inside every baby is a tightly wound spring. It is called the selfishness spring. Do babies ever think of anyone else except themselves? Do they ever stop crying because it is annoying to others?

All that babies ever think of is: me! me! me! They think that they are the center of the universe. The world exists to feed me, to change my diaper, to make funny goo-goo sounds at me.

For some people that spring unwinds a little as they grow up. They start to have consideration for other people's feelings. They learn to enjoy listening to others instead of just always talking about themselves.

Immature people love to find others with looser selfishness springs.

Mature people love to have looser springs.

end of short essay

As Fred walked through the campus toward the hospital, he thought about the ladder that the boy had climbed. *There should have been a sign on that ladder that read: Don't set this ladder up with a slope equal to 12. You may tip over backward.*

24'

2'

$$\text{slope} = \frac{24}{2}$$

Fred wondered whether the sign should have read: Make the slope as small as possible.

24'

36'

$$\text{slope} = \frac{24}{36}$$

He realized that this would also be dangerous. The ladder could slip out.

He decided that the sign should read:

> Do not make the slope too large or too small.

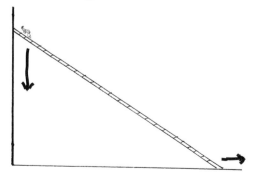

Your Turn to Play

The fraction $\frac{24}{36}$ can be reduced to make it easier to look at.

The rule for **reducing fractions** is that you can divide the top and the bottom of the fraction by the same number.

Both 24 and 36 are even numbers. The number 2 will divide into both of them evenly.

$24 \div 2 = 12$ and $36 \div 2 = 18$.

So $\frac{24}{36}$ is equal to $\frac{12}{18}$

1. Reduce $\frac{12}{18}$ as far as you can.

2. Reduce $\frac{6}{8}$

3. Reduce $\frac{10}{20}$

4. This is a whole pie.   This is $\frac{1}{3}$ of a pie.

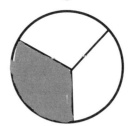

Draw pictures for your answers to problems 1, 2, and 3.

·······**ANSWERS**·······

1. Since 12 and 18 are both even numbers, we can divide them both by 2.

$$\frac{12}{18} = \frac{6}{9}$$

We can further reduce $\frac{6}{9}$ since both 6 and 9 are evenly divisible by 3.

$$\frac{6}{9} = \frac{2}{3}$$

(We originally started with $\frac{24}{36}$ and have reduced it down to $\frac{2}{3}$ which is a lot easier to look at than $\frac{24}{36}$)

2. Dividing top and bottom by 2, $\frac{6}{8}$ becomes $\frac{3}{4}$

3. Dividing top and bottom by 10, $\frac{10}{20}$ becomes $\frac{1}{2}$

4.

$$\frac{2}{3}$$

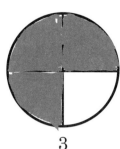

$$\frac{3}{4}$$

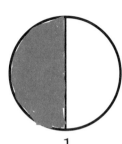

$$\frac{1}{2}$$

Chapter Fourteen
To the Hospital

Fred headed in the main entrance of the hospital. He politely waited until the nurse got off the phone.

After she finished her phone call, she still did not say hello to him. Of course, it might have been that she couldn't see him.

He knocked on the front of her desk.

She leaned over and saw him. She asked, "How may I help you? Are you sick?"

"No I'm not sick. I'm looking for a friend of mine who fell off a ladder. He's an actor."

She smiled. "I can tell you are also an actor."

Fred realized that he was still wearing a big hat with a feather in it. He said, "I used to be an actor. Can you tell me which room my friend is in?"

Three Possible Answers
to
"Can you tell me which room he is in?"

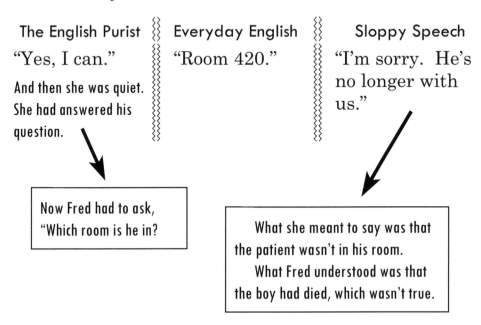

The English Purist

"Yes, I can."

And then she was quiet. She had answered his question.

Now Fred had to ask, "Which room is he in?

Everyday English

"Room 420."

Sloppy Speech

"I'm sorry. He's no longer with us."

What she meant to say was that the patient wasn't in his room.
What Fred understood was that the boy had died, which wasn't true.

Fred headed up to the fourth floor and down the hall to room 420. There was no one in the room.

A nurse walked in and said, "They are taking pictures of him in x-ray right now. He's got a bumpy on his head, and they are checking it out."

Fred responded, "Yes, it's important to investigate possible complications such as subarachnoid, subdural, or extradural hemorrhages in connection with significant trauma to the head."

(Fred is not your average five-year-old who refers to a cut or a scrape as an ouch, a hurty, a boo-boo, or an owie.)

When the nurse left the room, Fred looked at the patient's chart. Name: John Doe.* Age: 20. Weight: 73 g.

This is goofy, Fred thought. *Nobody's weighs 73 grams. A gram is the weight of a large paper clip.*

I bet they meant that he weighs 73 kg.

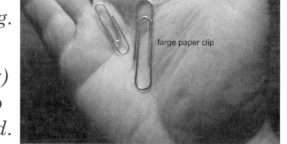

large paper clip

A kilogram (kg) is 1000 grams. Kilo means one thousand.

*A kilogram is a little bit more than two pounds.***

Fred weighs 37 pounds, which is about 17 kilograms.

---

* John Doe is the name used for a male whose real name is not known. For females, Jane Doe is used.

** For those dying to know, a kilogram is about 2.205 pounds.

As a fraction, 2.205 is equal to $2\frac{205}{1000}$

After waiting for a couple of minutes, the boy came back from getting x-rays. Fred told the nurse that 73 g did not look right.

She said, "Oh!" and corrected his chart. She wrote: Weight: *73 mg* and left the room.

This was even worse.

73 mg means 73 milligrams. A milligram is a thousandth of gram. It would take 1,000 milligrams to equal one gram.

Fred took a penny and put a grain of salt where Lincoln could look at it. A grain of salt weighs about one mg.

> *milli* = one thousandth
> *kilo* = one thousand

A meter is a little longer than a yard. (≈39 inches, where ≈ means *approximately equal to*.)

A millimeter is about the size of a period.

A kilometer is a thousand meters, which is a little over a half mile.*

---

* When you work with fractions in *Life of Fred: Fractions*, we might say that a kilometer is about $\frac{5}{8}$ of a mile. When you work with decimals in *Life of Fred: Decimals and Percents,* we might say that a kilometer is approximately 0.6214 miles.

The boy lay* in bed very quietly. Fred stood on a chair so that he could be seen by the boy.

The boy asked, "How is the play going? The doc looked at my x-rays and said that everything is okay. I'll just need to take it easy for a couple of days."

Fred told him that the director could not manage with so few people and that he had canceled the play.

Your Turn to Play

1. How much would a kilodollar (also known as a kilobuck) be?

2. If you got an allowance of one kilodollar each year, roughly, how much would that be each week? There are 52 weeks in a year.

3. Some people say, "I'll be back in a minute."

Suppose someone said, "I'll be back in a kilominute." Roughly, how many hours would that be?

4. Reduce the fraction $\dfrac{10}{12}$

5. In the expression 4^3, which number is the exponent?

6. $\sum\limits_{i=7}^{9} 9i = ?$

---

* Not *laid!* If he were a chicken, he could have laid eggs in bed.

........ANSWERS........

1. A kilodollar would be a thousand dollars ($1,000).

2. If you get $1,000 in one year (52 weeks), to find out how much that would be each week, you would divide. If you were not sure whether to add, subtract, multiply, or divide, then restate the problem with simple numbers. Suppose you get $20 in 4 weeks, how much would you get in one week? Five dollars. You divided.

$$
\begin{array}{r}
19\text{ R }12 \\
52\overline{)1000} \\
\underline{52} \\
480 \\
\underline{468} \\
12
\end{array}
$$

Roughly, $19 per week

3. With the same reasoning as the previous problem:

$$
\begin{array}{r}
16\text{ R }40 \\
60\overline{)1000} \\
\underline{60} \\
400 \\
\underline{360} \\
40
\end{array}
$$

A kilominute is roughly 16 hours.

4. We can divide the top and bottom of $\frac{10}{12}$ by 2.
    $\frac{10}{12}$ reduces to $\frac{5}{6}$

5. In the expression 4^3, 3 is the exponent.

6. $\sum\limits_{i=7}^{9} 9i = 9(7) + 9(8) + 9(9) = 63 + 72 + 81.$

$$
\begin{array}{r}
63 \\
72 \\
\underline{81} \\
216
\end{array}
$$

Chapter Fifteen
Zorba the Fred

Fred offered the boy his best wishes for a speedy recovery and asked if there was anything he could do for him before he left.

The boy asked Fred to turn on the radio that was beside his bed. It blared out the newest hit song.

Oh, sweetie, lovie,
  honey bunch,
I am your math book,
  yeah, yeah, yeah.
You are the one,
  boppa, boppa, twing, twing,
Who solves all my problems.

Fred waved goodbye and left. He couldn't shout over the music.

Even when Fred was outside the hospital, he could still hear You are the arsonist, ching, gloppa, gooey / Who sets my heart on fire.

In the old days, Fred thought, *hospitals, libraries, and waiting rooms were much quieter.* Of course, in Fred's case, the old days meant five years ago.

The words ching, gloppa, gooey kept running through Fred's head. He added a fourth word so that he could play the Which One Is Not Like the Others game. Being a math guy, he added the word *million*.

ching   gloppa   gooey   million

The game was to find a way that each of these is not like the other.

Ching is the only monosyllabic* word.

Gloppa is the only word containing the letter *a*.

Gooey is the only word that reminds people of warm, cheesy pizza.

Million is the only math word.

Fred liked to play games like that because they were fun.

Often, Fred would break out into singing at this point. Tonight was different. He decided to dance. He had recently seen the movie "Zorba,

---

* Monosyllabic = has one syllable. The prefix *mono* means "one."
     (for artists) monochrome = art done in only one color
     (for actors) monodrama = a play with only one performer
     (for writers) monograph = a writing on a single subject
     (for Stan) monophagous = eating only one kind of food (pizza)
     (for poets) monostich = a poem consisting of only one line

the Greek," and remembered how Zorba taught his friend to dance.

Fred hopped once on his left foot. Then twice on his right foot. Three times on his left foot. Four times on his right foot.

Fred thought, *Will I ever hop an odd number of times on my right foot? No. That was an easy question.*

Then Fred hopped once on his left foot. Twice on his right. Four times on his left foot. Eight times on his right.

This was Fred's famous Double Dance. Each time you switch feet, you double the number of hops.

Fred thought, *If each hop moved me forward one inch, how long will it be before I'm hopping a whole mile on one foot?*

First, he needed to figure out how many inches in a mile. One mile is 5,280 feet. Each foot is 12 inches.

$$
\begin{array}{r}
5280 \\
\times\ \ \ \ 12 \\
\hline
10560 \\
5280\ \ \ \\
\hline
63360
\end{array}
$$

Please check to make sure the multiplication is correct.

There are 63,360 inches in a mile.

Now, to figure out how many times he would have to switch feet in his Double Dance before he would hop at least 63,360" on one foot.

On the left foot	1" hopped
After 1 switch	2" hopped on right foot
After 2 switches	4" hopped on left foot
After 3 switches	8"
4 switches	16"
5 switches	32"
6	64"
7	128"
8	256"
9	512"
10	1,024"
11	2,048"
12	4,096"
13	8,192"
14	16,384"
15	32,768
16	65,536"

It would be a short dance. After he switched feet 16 times, he would be hopping over a mile on his left foot.

When Fred taught, he would have his whole class do the Double Dance, and he would write on the board: $2^{16} = 65,536$.

Fred liked to invent games or puzzles to keep his mind sharp. He called them brain sharpeners.

<hr>

Your Turn to Sharpen Your Brain

The whole numbers are {0, 1, 2, 3, 4, 5, 6, . . .}.

1. If x is an even whole number, what can you say about x + 1?

2. If x is a whole number, must 10x have two digits?

3. Is it possible to name a whole number x so that the number of digits in x is greater than x itself?

    For example, if x were 674, then the number of digits in x—which is 3—is not greater than 674.

4. If x is a whole number, must 10x be even?

[question for artists]

5. If A, B, and C are three points on a map, will it always be true that going from A to B and then from B to C will be longer than going from A directly to C?

<hr>

........ANSWERS ....

1. If x is an even number, such as 0, 2, 4, or 678, then x + 1 will be an odd number, such as 1, 3, 5, or 679.

2. If x is a whole number, such as 1, 2, 3, 4, . . . 8, or 9, then certainly 10x would have two digits. However, if x is any other whole number, 10x won't have two digits.

    For example, if x = 0, then 10x (which is 0) has one digit. If x = 10, then 10x (which is 100) has three digits. If x = 48,293, then 10x (which is 482,930) has 6 digits.

3. There is only one whole number where the number of its digits is greater than the number itself. Zero has one digit.

4. If x is a whole number, then 10x must have a zero in the one's place. For example, if x = 74, then 10x = 740. (There is a 0 in the one's place, 4 in the ten's place, and 7 in the hundred's place.) Any number ending in zero will be evenly divisible by two. Hence, 10x must be even.

5. If you just put three points on a map at random, then it will be longer going from A to B and then from B to C, than just going directly from A to C.

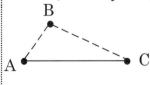

However, the question asks if that is *always* true. It will not be true in the very special case that B is directly on the road from A to C.

Chapter Sixteen
A New Way of Counting

The night grew cold.
The hopping old.
He stopped the dance
And headed to France.*

It was time to head back to his office. It was getting late. As he walked by the Millard Fillmore Police Station, he could see lights shining from rooms on the third floor.

Someone must be working late tonight, Fred thought.

Fred started to daydream about a new way of counting. The old-fashioned way of counting was good for counting

---

* This is called an **epigraph** (EP-pa-graf). Epigraphs are quotations at the beginning of chapters.

This particular epigraph is a poem that Fred wrote. He had been reading Henry Wadsworth Longfellow's *The Song of Hiawatha*:

> Never more in human figure
> Shall you search for now adventures;
> Never more with jest and laughter
> Dance the dust and leaves in whirlwinds;
> But above there in heavens
> You shall soar and sail in circles. . . .

Writing poetry looked like it would be fun. He was going to call himself Fred Shortfellow.

When he was writing the poem for this epigraph, Fred had trouble finding a word to rhyme with *dance.*

He had tried: He stopped the jump / And fell in the dump.

He had tried: He came to a halt / And had a chocolate malt.

He had tried: And at the end / He couldn't bend.

birthday candles. The candles were standing very still, and you could just say, "1, 2, 3, 4, 5, 6, 7" and count them all.

But, Fred thought, *suppose I were a librarian, and I was told to keep track of how many questions I was asked during the day. I might get three questions in a row and then have to wait fifteen minutes before the next question. It would be hard to remember. I could easily lose count.*

Your Questions Answered

Fred first thought of writing down 1, when the first question was asked. Then when the second question was asked, he could cross off the 1 and write a 2. At the end of the day, it might look like: 1̶ 2̶ 3̶ 4 5̶ 6̶ 7 8̶ 9̶ 1̶0̶ 1̶1̶ 12. That seemed like a lot of work.

Instead, why not just write a tally mark when each person asks a question? The problem is that at the end of the day your tally marks might look like: | | | | | | | | | | | | | | | | | | | | | | | | | | and you would have to go back and count all the marks.

The whole point of math is to make things easier.

Instead, Fred made his tally marks in groups of five: ⵉ⵰ ⵉ⵰ ⵉ⵰ ⵉ⵰ ‖. You could count by fives and see that there are 22 tallies.

Then he imagined that he would have to keep track of the various types of questions he might be asked as a librarian.

At the end of another day, his tally marks might look like this:

Where can I find books about . . . ? ⵉ⵰ |

How many books can I check out? |||

Where is the bathroom? |||

He could report that information as a bar graph.

He could report that information as a pie chart.

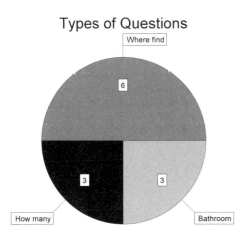

Fred arrived at the Math Building. It is amazing how fast time goes by when you are dancing or daydreaming.

He headed up the stairs and down the hallway. He was expecting to see the nine vending machines—five on one side and four on the other. They were all gone! Those machines had been there ever since Fred started teaching at KITTENS years ago.

When he got to his office at the end of the hall, his schedule of classes had been removed from the door.

Fred Gauss
—room 314—

8–9 Arithmetic
9–10 Beginning Algebra
10–11 Advanced Algebra
11–noon Geometry
noon–1 Trigonometry
1–2 Calculus
2–3 Statistics
3–3:05 Break
3:05–4 Linear Algebra
4–5 Seminar in Biology, Economics, Physics, Set Theory, Topology, and Metamathematics.

◄------------------ Gone!

Instead of his class schedule, there was a giant poster of a German castle and a little sign:

Prof. Heide von Hilfe
German Studies
German 1   M–F 8-9
German 2   M–F 9-10
German 3   M–F 10-11
German 4   M–F 11-noon

Fred panicked. His thoughts raced.

☹ *What have they done with Kingie?*

☹ *Have I been fired?*

☹ *Where will I sleep tonight?*

Could you ever imagine a worse time for a . . .

Your Turn to Play

1. Write 18 using tally marks.

2. Looking at the pie chart, what fraction of the questions concerned the bathroom?

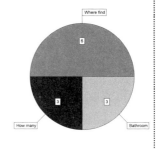

3. Fred had made 12 tally marks. Three of them had been bathroom-related questions.

    Three out of 12 can be expressed as $\dfrac{3}{12}$

Reduce that fraction.

4. Roughly, how many years are two kilodays? (There are approximately 365 days in a year.)

5. Fred normally weighs 37 pounds. Standing in front of Prof. Heide's door, he lost 2 ounces. (It was a combination of tears and sweat.) How much does he now weigh?

. . . . . . .ANSWERS . . . .

1. ⵏⵏⵏ ⵏⵏⵏ ⵏⵏⵏ |||

2. One-fourth ($\frac{1}{4}$) of the questions concerned the bathroom.

3. To reduce $\frac{3}{12}$ we divide top and bottom by 3.

$$\frac{3}{12} \;=\; \frac{3 \div 3}{12 \div 3} \;=\; \frac{1}{4}$$

(Problems 2 and 3 are related.)

4. Two kilodays would be 2,000 days.

Two kilodays is
roughly 5 years.

$$
\begin{array}{r}
5 \text{ R } 175 \\
365\overline{)2000} \\
1825 \\
\hline
175
\end{array}
$$

5.   37 lbs.

$$
\begin{array}{r}
37 \text{ lbs.} \\
- \qquad 2 \text{ oz.} \\
\hline
\end{array}
$$

$$
\begin{array}{rr}
36 & \\
\cancel{37} \text{ lbs.} & 16 \text{ oz.} \\
- & 2 \text{ oz.} \\
\hline
36 \text{ lbs.} & 14 \text{ oz.}
\end{array}
$$

Chapter Seventeen
Heidi's Office

It was after nine o'clock at night. Fred's day had started at 3:40 in the morning when he was awoken by his leaking fish tank. He had not taken a nap all day.

This is a bad ending for a long day, Fred thought. *Did I do something wrong, and have they given my office to Heidi von Hilfe?*

He knocked on the door. There was no answer. This was not surprising since it was Sunday night.

He tried opening the door. It was locked. He tried his key but it wouldn't work.

And they have also changed the lock!

He wondered if this is what it felt like to be homeless. He took out his handkerchief and wiped his eyes and blew his nose.[*]

After he put his handkerchief away, he looked at the door: room 214. His office was 314. IIe had only climbed one flight of stairs instead of two. He was on the wrong floor. An easy mistake to make when you are really tired.

---

[*] These are not commutative. You don't want to wipe your eyes with a handkerchief after you have blown your nose in it.

He walked down the hallway with no vending machines, climbed a flight of stairs, went down the hallway with nine vending machines, and entered his office.

Kingie was just finishing up his 14th oil painting. On a white board in back of his easel he kept track of how many paintings he did each day.

Kingie asked, "How did your speech go at the Math and Pizza Conference?"

That seemed like so long ago for Fred, and yet it was only about five hours earlier. Fred said, "My whole speech was seven words long but everyone really liked it."

Kingie is much more of a businessman than Fred. $400 for seven words.

He quickly computed . . .

that Fred had been paid
a little over $57 for each word
that he had spoken.

$$57 \frac{1}{7}$$
$$7\overline{)400}$$
$$\underline{35}$$
$$50$$
$$\underline{49}$$
$$1$$

Fred's salary for teaching at KITTENS is $500 per month.

A person's income
does not depend
only on the number
of hours worked.

Your income does depend on . . .

1. How long you work.

Students in American government schools are in the classroom about 180 days per year. That's less than half of the days in a year.

Japan has a 243-day school year.[*]

$$\begin{array}{r} 243 \\ -\,180 \\ \hline 63 \end{array}$$

2. How hard you work.

Some people get twice as much done as others in the same amount of time. Which workers will get promotions and raises?

3. How much *real* education you have.

Getting a college degree does not equal a real education. It makes a significant difference which major you choose in college.

4. How easily you can be replaced by others.

If you are doing a job that almost anybody can do, then there are always others who are willing to work for less than you. Become a brain surgeon, a mathematician, or a nuclear engineer and you won't have to worry about being replaced by robots or foreign competition.

---

[*] The World Economic Forum ranks American students 48th in math. Kids from 47 countries beat American kids in math.

5. What country you live in.

It is not how much you make that counts; it is how much you get to keep. Taxes make a big difference.

In the United States, the top federal income tax is currently 35%. The top state income tax is 11%. The top sales tax is 10%. TOTAL = 56%* (56 percent means $56 out of every $100.)

In Denmark, the top income tax is 67%, and the VAT (which is like a sales tax) is 25%. TOTAL = 92%.

If you want to keep a lot of the money you earn, Switzerland's top income tax rate is 13%, and the top VAT is 8%. TOTAL = 23%.

Money is nice, especially if you like to do things like eat or wear clothes. On the other hand, there is some point in getting wealthy at which, if someone hands you an extra thousand dollars, it won't change how you live at all.

A hundred years from now, if someone offers you a brand new car, a mansion, a ton of cash, you won't show the slightest bit of interest.

---

* These numbers are rounded to the nearest percent.

Your Turn to Play

1. Fred teaches from 8 a.m. to 5 p.m. each day. How many hours is that?

2. How many hours per week does he teach? (His classes are held Monday through Friday.)

3. After deductions for federal income tax, state income tax, and Social Security, he receives $90 per week. How much does Fred receive per hour of teaching? (Use the results of the previous problem.)

4. Take the number of days in a year. Multiply it by six. Then add 9,398,982. Then multiply by 777. Then subtract 2,900,185. Then multiply by zero. What is your final answer? (You need not show all your work.)

When Fred was pretending to be a librarian and answering questions, he might have written down each question. His list might have looked like:

1. Where can I find a copy of Moby Dick? 2. Where is the bathroom? 3. How many books can I check out? 4. Where can I find a book on cooking pigeons? 5. Does the library have any Life of Fred books? etc.

Suppose someone asks you how many questions are there in his list from question 40 to question 47?

If you answer "7," you have made an error that lots of people make. Let's count them.

40	41	42	43	44	45	46	47
1	2	3	4	5	6	7	8

There are seven steps from 40 to 47 but there are eight members of the set {40, 41, 42, 43, 44, 45, 46, 47}.

·······ANSWERS·······

1. From 8 a.m. to noon is 4 hours.

   From noon to 5 p.m. is 5 hours.

He teaches 9 hours per day.

2. He teaches 9 hours per day, five days per week. He teaches 45 hours per week.

3. **He receives $90 for 45 hours of work.** If you don't know whether to add, subtract, multiply, or divide, restate the problem with simpler numbers. Suppose he is paid $6 for 2 hours of work. That would be $3 per hour. You divided.

$$45\overline{)\,90}^{\,2}$$ He is paid $2 per hour of teaching.

Time Out!

Is Fred happy with this situation? Yes! Fred does not suffer from the biggest happiness killer: envy.

Envy is being unhappy because of what other people have.

In many state universities today, some of the math professors receive over $100,000 a year. They teach less than half of the days of the year, and teach only six or nine hours per week. But Fred doesn't compare himself with others.

He is happy. Not many five-year-olds get $90 a week to spend as they wish. He is doing exactly what he wants to do, which is teaching math. He loves what he is doing.

4. This is the easiest problem in the whole book. Whenever you multiply any number by zero, the answer will always be zero.

Chapter Eighteen
Kingie's Computer

Kingie took his 14th painting off the easel and began cleaning up his brushes and pallet. There are few things as satisfying as a full day of creative work.

His cell phone rang. It was the Getty Museum. They asked if any of his paintings were available.

Kingie told them that the first dozen had already been sold but the last two were still for sale. They agreed on a price.

A man from the museum would come tomorrow to pick up the last two.

Kingie entered the day's sales into his computer :

```
sales:

$1900, $1900, $2000, $1900,
$2000, $2100, $2000, $2000,
$2000, $2000, $2100, $2500,
$4600, $4700.
```

Then Kingie typed in: `Please average these.`

The computer asked: `Which average would you like?`

Kingie didn't know, so he typed: `Give me all of them.`

The computer said: `Okay.`

First, it found the **median average**. It lined up the numbers from smallest to largest and picked the one in the middle.

`1900, 1900, 1900, 2000, 2000, 2000, 2000, 2000,`
`2000, 2100, 2100, 2500, 4600, 4700`

`The median average is 2000.`

Second, it found the **mean average**. It added up the fourteen numbers (=`33,700`) and divided by `14`. `The mean average is`
`2407.14285714285714285714285714285` `429.`

Kingie mentally rounded that off to $2407.

Third, the computer found the **mode average**. The mode average is the most common number. `The mode average is 2000.`

Kingie patted the computer on its monitor head and turned it off.

Fred grabbed his toiletries (toothbrush, toothpaste, floss, soap, and towel—but no comb or deodorant) and headed down the hallway to the restroom.

He passed the vending machine that sold
Jelly Stomach Jelly Beans and
recalled the survey that had
been taken of KITTENS
students last week. They had
asked 100 students, "How many
Jelly Stomach Jelly Beans have
you eaten in the last week?"

The KITTEN Caboodle
newspaper reported the results:
0, 0, 0, 0, 0, 0, 0, 0, 0, 0, 0, 0, 0, 0, 0, 0, 0, 0, 0,
0, 0, 0, 0, 0, 0, 0, 0, 0, 0, 0, 0, 0, 0, 0, 0, 0, 0, 0, 0,
0, 0, 0, 0, 0, 0, 0, 0, 0, 0, 0, 0, 0, 0, 0, 0, 0, 0, 0, 0,
0, 0, 0, 0, 0, 0, 0, 0, 0, 0, 0, 0, 0, 0, 0, 0, 0, 0, 0, 0,
0, 0, 0, 0, 0, 0, 0, 0, 0, 0, 0, 0, 0, 0, 0, 0, 0, 0, 0,
827,900.

One student had eaten 827,900 of them in
the last week. The newspaper did not mention
the name of that student but everyone on
campus knew who he was.*

The paper reported that the average
student ate zero Jelly Stomach Jelly Beans last
week. (They were using either the median or
the mode average.)

However, the company that made Jelly
Stomach Jelly Beans wanted to show that its
product was very popular with students. It used

---

* His name has three letters in it. The first letter is J. He is the boyfriend of Darlene.

the mean average. It added up the hundred numbers (= 827,900) and divided by one hundred. It advertised that students ate an average of 8,279 Jelly Stomach Jelly Beans last week.

The advertisement was true but it wasn't the whole truth.

Fred headed into the restroom and put down his toiletries. He washed his hands and pulled out three inches of floss.

This was a brand new container of Duck brand floss. Fred figured that he would be using it for years.

3 Miles of Floss!

As he flossed, he computed how much was left in the container.

$$
\begin{array}{r}
3 \text{ miles} \\
- \qquad\qquad 3 \text{ inches} \\
\hline
\end{array}
$$

He borrowed one mile.

$$
\begin{array}{r}
2 \\
\cancel{3} \text{ miles} \quad 5280 \text{ feet} \\
- \qquad\qquad\qquad\qquad\qquad 3 \text{ inches} \\
\hline
\end{array}
$$

He borrowed one foot.

$$\begin{array}{rll}
\overset{2}{\cancel{3}} \text{ miles} & \overset{5279}{\cancel{5280}} \text{ feet} & 12 \text{ inches}\\
 & & 3 \text{ inches}\\
\hline
2 \text{ miles} & 5279 \text{ feet} & 9 \text{ inches.}
\end{array}$$

He had 2 miles, 5,279 feet, 9 inches left.

Your Turn to Play

1. Subtract three seconds from three years.

2. Write 42 using tally marks.

3. The whole numbers are {0, 1, 2, 3, 4, 5, . . .}.

   If x is an even whole number, what can you say about x + 40?

4. Reduce the fraction $\dfrac{20}{30}$

5. {6, 7, 8} ∪ {7, 8} = ?

   {6, 7, 8} ∩ {7, 8} = ?

   {6, 7, 8} − {7, 8} = ?

6. Fred bought his Duck brand floss for 63¢ and paid a dollar. Count back the change.

. . . . ANSWERS . . . .

1.   3 years
    −   3 seconds
    ─────────────────────────────────

    2
    3̶ years   365 days
    −   3 seconds
    ─────────────────────────────────

                        364
    2 years   3̶6̶5̶ days   24 hours
    −   3 seconds
    ─────────────────────────────────

                                    23
    2 years   364 days   2̶4̶ hours   60 minutes
    −   3 seconds
    ─────────────────────────────────

                                              59
    2 years   364 days   23 hours   6̶0̶ minutes   60 seconds
    −   3 seconds
    ─────────────────────────────────
    2 years   364 days   23 hours   59 minutes   57 seconds

2. Ⱦ Ⱦ Ⱦ Ⱦ Ⱦ Ⱦ Ⱦ Ⱦ ||

3. If x is an even whole number, then x + 40 must also be an even whole number. For example, if x = 8, then x + 40 is 48. If x = 60, then x + 40 is 100.

4. Twenty and 30 are both evenly divisible by 10.

$$\frac{20}{30} = \frac{20 \div 10}{30 \div 10} = \frac{2}{3}$$

5. {6, 7, 8} ∪ {7, 8} = {6, 7, 8}

   {6, 7, 8} ∩ {7, 8} = {7, 8}

   {6, 7, 8} − {7, 8} = {6}

6. 63 → 64 → 65 → 75 → one dollar.

Chapter Nineteen
A Day Older

Fred brushed his twenty deciduous teeth. He checked to see if any of his incisors* were getting loose. He was still too young to start getting his adult teeth.

He checked his upper lip to see if he needed to start shaving. He put some foam from the toothpaste on his upper lip to make a pretend moustache. He would have to wait until he was a teenager, before he got some real facial hair.

He washed his face, gathered up his toiletries, and headed back toward his office.

In the hallway, he thought of his Duck brand dental floss and wondered, *Ducks never get moustaches. Why is that?*

Then he realized that ducks don't have hair at all.

Maybe I'm a duck! How do I know that I am not a duck?

---

* Incisors are the flat teeth in the front of the mouth. They are used for cutting. Whenever Fred thought about his incisors, he thought about what he might look like if he were a beaver.

Fred was pretty tired and crazy thoughts roiled* in his head: *I have no hair. My nose is like a duck's bill. I'm short as a duck. I can say, "Quack!"*

Then he remembered:

Ducks Can't Do Math.

He felt much better.

He counted aloud by twelves as he entered his office: "12, 24, 36, 48, 60, 72, 84, 96, 108." He knew that once you can count by twelves, it becomes pretty easy to learn the twelve times table.

Kingie was getting ready for bed. Fred told him, "I can count by twelves."

Kingie told him, "Anybody can do that. One dozen, two dozen, three dozen, four dozen."

Fred felt very silly. His doll had outsmarted him.

Kingie said goodnight and headed into his fort. Fred could hear him playing softly on his piano. That was something Kingie often did before he headed for bed.

---

* Roiled is like boiled, except there is no heat involved. Roiled = stirred up, disturbed, made turbulent.

Fred got on his nightclothes, turned off the light, and walked to the window. The sky was black and filled with stars.

So many things had happened today. The leaking fish tank. Throwing his sleeping bag out of the window. Jogging southeast and seeing all those houses. Meeting Betty and Alexander who were also out jogging. Being a cowboy with a lasso. Carrie at Sunday school. Finding out about bees and honey cards. Thinking about becoming an apiarist. Learning from Kingie the three questions to ask when starting a business. Getting rejected for a credit card. Joe getting the sleeping bag out of the tree. Getting Joe out of the tree. . . .

And those were just the things that happened before noon.

Fred wondered what it would be like when he got really old, say 30 years old, and he looked back on his whole life.

What would be important: the things he did—or would it be the people whose lives he touched?

The stars were getting a little blurry. He rubbed his eyes and headed to his sleeping bag. He offered a prayer of thankfulness and fell asleep.

Index

It's time to celebrate!

You have just finished the *Life of Fred Elementary Series*.

We began the series at 5 a.m. on Monday in *Life of Fred: Apples*. Fred woke up, climbed out of his sleeping bag, and played with seven pencils. It is now six days later on Sunday evening. Fred has headed back to his sleeping bag and has fallen asleep.

What a week this has been! If we pick out one of the ten books a random, say *Life of Fred: Edgewood,* we can think back to some of the things you have learned in that book:

Dangling participles, Concurrent Lines, Christina Rossetti's "A Chill," Dealing with Troubles, Parallel Lines, Trapezoids, Right Angles, Facing Things You Don't Want to Do, Functions, Rhombuses, Constant Functions, Tripoli, Eritrea, Median Average, Writing Larger Numbers with Commas, Using Logarithms to Solve $2^x = 5$, Birdie Rule for Logarithms, Finding Approximate values for log 5 on a Calculator, Bar Graphs, Math Poems, >, Couplets in Poetry, *Strait* does not mean *Straight*, Judging People by their Size, If Fred Were an Author, Numbers that Add to 8, 10, and 12, Population of the Earth, State Income Tax Rates as Percents, Definition of Polka Dots, Parallelograms, Rows and Columns of a Matrix, the Four Kinds of Sentences: Declarative, Interrogative, Imperative, and Exclamation, Pronouns, Quarter of an Hour, Importance of Seat Belts, Small, Medium, and Large Mistakes, *Busted* vs. *Broken*, Half Dozen, Gibbous Moons, Dusk, Two Kinds of Knowledge Errors, Firearm Safety, Symptoms of Hypothermia, Voluntary and Involuntary Actions of the Body, Lorentz Contraction, International Date Line, Treatment of Hypothermia, the Addition Game Using Playing Cards, *Alright* Is Not a Word, Playing Guess-A-Function, Six Examples of Functions: Add, Subtract, Multiply, Divide, Tangent, and Derivative, One Way to Feel Lonely, What It Means to Matriculate.

Your adventures with Fred have just begun. In the books listed on the next page, we will continue with the life of our five-year-old. He is going to turn six in algebra.

In the giant 544-page book, *Life of Fred: Calculus*, you can read about the day that Fred was born and about his mother and father. You will learn how he got his job at KITTENS University.

You will also learn some math. Right now, you can figure out a value of x that will make $x + 3 = 7$ true.

In beginning algebra, you will be able to find two different values of x that make $4x^2 + 9x + 2 = 0$ true.

In advanced algebra, you will be able to find a value of x that makes $3^x = 8$ true.

In trigonometry, you will be able to find five different values of x that make $x^5 = 1$ true.

There are a lot of fun times ahead.

Polka Dot Publishing

Life of Fred: Fractions	$19
Life of Fred: Decimals and Percents	$19
Life of Fred: Pre-Algebra 1 with Biology	$29
Life of Fred: Pre-Algebra 2 with Economics	$29
Life of Fred: Beginning Algebra	$29
Fred's Home Companion: Beginning Algebra	$14
Life of Fred: Advanced Algebra	$29
Fred's Home Companion: Advanced Algebra	$14
Life of Fred: Geometry	$39
answer key *Life of Fred: Geometry* (paper)	$6
Life of Fred: Trigonometry	$29
Fred's Home Companion: Trigonometry	$14
Life of Fred: Calculus	$39
answer key *Life of Fred: Calculus* (paper)	$6
Life of Fred: Statistics	$39
answer key *Life of Fred: Statistics* (paper)	$6
Life of Fred: Linear Algebra	$49
answer key *Life of Fred: Linear Algebra* (paper)	$6

Two years of college calculus.

A year of college statistics.

Linear algebra is a math course that is required of almost all math majors in college. It is usually studied after calculus.

Order through our website: PolkaDotPublishing.com